Leaping into Literature

D1538174

A Guide to Enhance Your Primary Literature Program

by
Laurie Chapin and Ellen Flegenheimer-Riggle

illustrated by Laurie Chapin

Cover by Jeff Van Kanegan

Copyright © Good Apple, Inc., 1990

Good Apple, Inc.
1204 Buchanan St., Box 299
Carthage, IL 62321-0299

GA1164

Copyright © Good Apple, Inc., 1990

ISBN No. 0-86653-561-6

Printing No. 98

Good Apple, Inc.
1204 Buchanan St., Box 299
Carthage, IL 62321-0299

Dedicated

with love to

Cari

Andrew

Alyssia

Adrienne

Zachary

Dave

and

Frank . . .

Special thanks to
Kimberly Cloud

GA1164

Table of Contents

GA1164

Introduction

Leaping into Literature is a resource book that uses distinguished children's literature as a vehicle to encourage higher level thinking, problem solving, and creativity. Through lively discussion and creative activities, children's learning experiences in reading and language arts will be greatly enhanced. The ideas in the book provide a stimulus for the development of thoughts, experiences, and creative ideas. It is especially relevant for those children showing high aptitude in these areas.

Leaping into Literature focuses on the development of activities which are based on two different theories that emphasize skills essential to the above average learner. These theories include the characteristics of creativity: fluency, flexibility, originality, and elaboration, as well as Bloom's Taxonomy of thinking skills. Each activity is designed to challenge the children's abilities and encourage them to use those abilities to the fullest extent. The ideas will help children expand their minds by asking for new ideas, and encourage the students to be independent problem solvers.

Leaping into Literature provides concrete lessons and open-ended activities that teachers can use with an entire class, a small group, or on an individual basis. The book should be used in a manner best suited to the needs of the teacher and the students. It is hoped that these ideas will serve as a springboard to other adventures in creativity and enrich the reading experiences of young readers.

May *Leaping into Literature* provide the "magic" in your literature program.

Bloom's Taxonomy of Thinking

Knowledge: questions that ask one to recall information
questions that check the basic facts

Key Words: define, memorize, list, label, identify, show, recall, collect, recognize

Comprehension: questions that check one's understanding of the material

Key Words: describe, explain, dramatize, retell, identify

Application: questions that ask one to apply and use information in a new situation

Key Words: apply, experiment, show, solve, describe

Analysis: questions that ask one to break apart information and examine its separate parts and relationships

Key Words: connect, relate, arrange, analyze, compare, contrast

Synthesis: questions that ask one to use information in a new, creative and original way

Key Words: design, create, construct, imagine, suppose

Evaluation: questions that ask one to make judgements, with support, about the value of given information

Key Words: judge, debate, decide, criticize

GA1164

Creative Thinking Activities

Fluency: activities that ask one to produce a large quantity of ideas or responses

Flexibility: activities that ask one to think of alternative ideas or categories of ideas and to change one's way of thinking about a given situation

Originality: activities that ask one to produce unique and novel ideas and responses

Elaboration: activities that ask one to expand upon a single idea by adding detail or making changes to make it more interesting and complete

GA1164

Leaping into Literature Will . . .

- enhance your primary literature or whole language program

- introduce students to distinguished children's literature

- enhance students' higher level thinking skills

- encourage and expand students' creativity

- encourage students to look beyond the obvious

- promote a cooperative classroom environment

- involve students actively in the learning process

- provide the teacher with quality class discussion time

- provide the teacher with ideas from bulletin board displays

- provide the teacher with materials for the "already ready" student

- provide the teacher with learning center materials for independent study

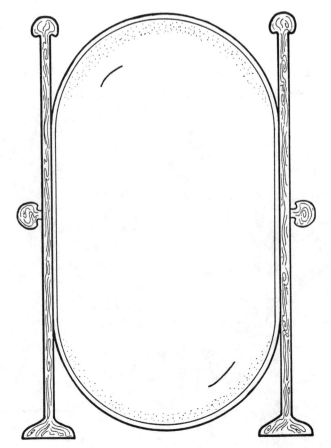

GA1164

Suggestions for Using This Book

Bloom's Questions

- Select all or some of the questions and activities for a whole group discussion, small group or paired discussion, or independent study.

- Create a comfortable atmosphere by accepting answers in a non-judgemental manner.

- Allow children ample time to respond to each question.

- Allow active participation from many children.

- Use blank shapes for making Bloom's Question cards. (See Blank Shape directions.)

HOW WOULD YOU SPEND YOUR DAY IN THE SNOW?

- Use blank shapes for recording children's individual responses to Bloom's Questions.

GA1164

Creative Thinking Activities

- Be accepting of all answers.

- Allow adequate discussion time for brainstorming to become fruitful.

- Allow adequate "wait time" for each answer.

- Create a class Brainstorming Book to record fluency activities. (Use large lined chart paper. Glue wrapping paper on the front for a colorful cover.)

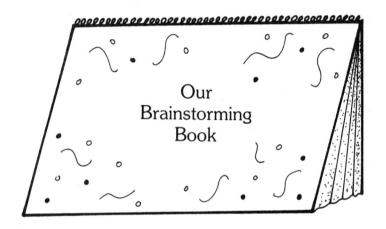

Our Brainstorming Book

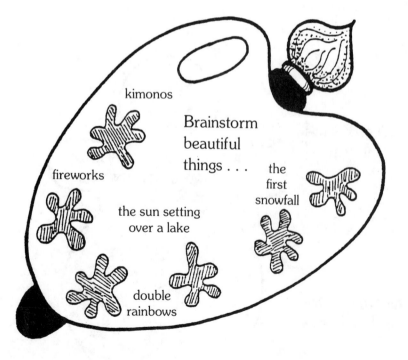

kimonos
Brainstorm beautiful things . . .
fireworks
the first snowfall
the sun setting over a lake
double rainbows

- Use blank shapes for making Creative Thinking Activity cards. (See Blank Shape directions.)

- Use blank shapes for recording children's individual responses to Creative Thinking Activities.

GA1164

Blank Shapes

- Reproduce blank shapes to make shape cards. Print the questions and activities on them. Use one question per shape. Laminate and assemble cards on a ring.

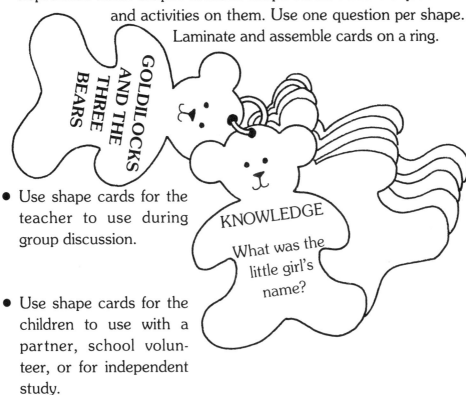

- Use shape cards for the teacher to use during group discussion.

- Use shape cards for the children to use with a partner, school volunteer, or for independent study.

- Use shape cards at a learning center. Display them with the book and activity sheets.

- Use shapes for a class book or an individual student's book.

- Reproduce shapes for children to record individual thoughts.

- Use shapes to create a bulletin board display.

GA1164

Activity Sheets

- An asterisk designates written or illustrated activities that include activity sheets.

- Use activity sheets as a bulletin board display.

- Use activity sheets to create a class book.

- Assemble by laminating a colorful cover.

- Attach students' work with:

  —plastic spiral binding

  —hole punch with notebook ring or yarn

  —staple

GA1164

ALEXANDER AND THE TERRIBLE, HORRIBLE, NO GOOD, VERY BAD DAY

Judith Viorst
Atheneum, NY, 1973

Alexander knows right from the start that he is going to have a very bad day. The book explores his terrible day.

BLOOM'S QUESTIONS

KNOWLEDGE
List three things that caused Alexander to have a terrible day.

COMPREHENSION
Why was Alexander angry with his teacher?

APPLICATION
Make suggestions to Alexander as to how he could have made his day better.

ANALYSIS
How is Alexander's bad day like a bad day that you have experienced? How is it different?

SYNTHESIS
Pretend Alexander had a terrific day. What happy events might have happened?

EVALUATION
Decide what event in the story was the most terrible. Tell why.

CREATIVE THINKING ACTIVITIES

FLUENCY
Brainstorm a long, long list of "terrible, horrible, no good, very bad" things.

FLEXIBILITY
Select what you think is the worst thing from your list and tell why it is the worst.

*ORIGINALITY
Create a magic potion that will get rid of a "terrible, horrible, no good, very bad day."

*ELABORATION
Elaborate on these pajamas so Alexander will be happy to wear them.

1

GA1164

AUSTRALIA

GA1164

Create a magic potion that will
get rid of a "terrible, horrible, no good,
very bad day."

_____

You Need

_____

_____

_____

_____

Then

_____

_____

_____

Chemist _____

GA1164

Elaborate on these pajamas so
Alexander will be happy to wear them.

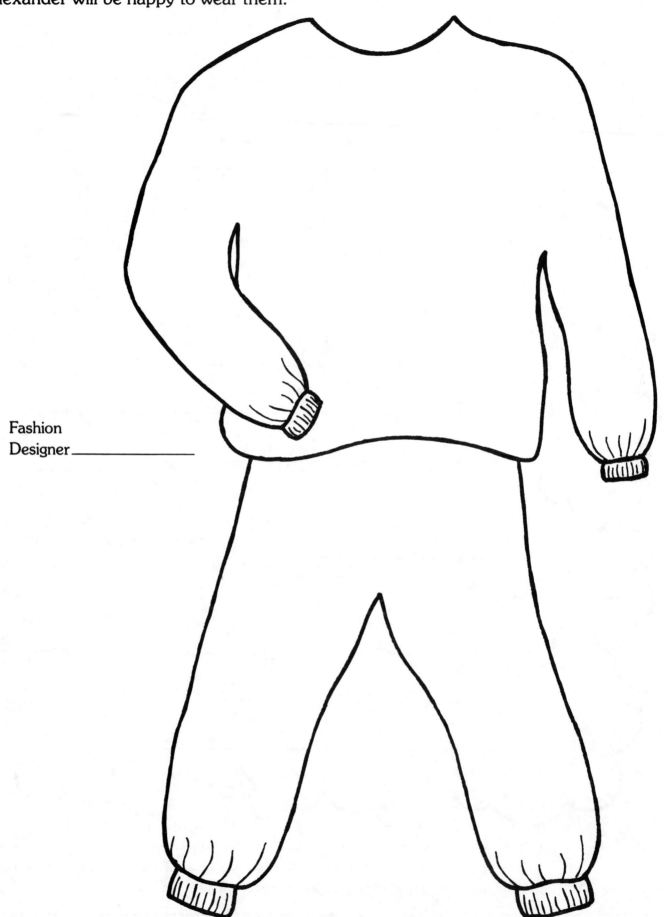

Fashion
Designer _____

4

ARTHUR'S CHRISTMAS COOKIES

Lillian Hoban
Harper & Row, NY, 1972

It is Christmas and Arthur decides to bake his very own Christmas present.

BLOOM'S QUESTIONS

KNOWLEDGE
Who does Arthur want to make a Christmas present for?

COMPREHENSION
Describe the troubles Arthur had in trying to make a gift for his parents.

APPLICATION
What would you do if you did not have any money to buy your parents a Christmas gift?

ANALYSIS
Compare Arthur's gift to Violet's gift. How are they alike? How are they different?

SYNTHESIS
Suppose the sugar cookies had turned out all right. How would this have changed the story?

EVALUATION
Judge whether Arthur's Christmas cookies were a good present for his parents. Why or why not?

CREATIVE THINKING ACTIVITIES

FLUENCY
List all the cookie words you know or can find.

FLEXIBILITY
Think of some different uses for cookies besides eating them.

*ORIGINALITY
Take a survey to see which cookie is most popular among your friends.

*ELABORATION
Elaborate on Arthur's cookie shapes. Decorate them so they are ready to hang on the Christmas tree. (Cut them out, punch a hole in the top, string them with yarn, and hang on a classroom tree or cut out and invent a name for each cookie. Glue each cookie on a separate page and staple into a cookie book.)

GA1164

6

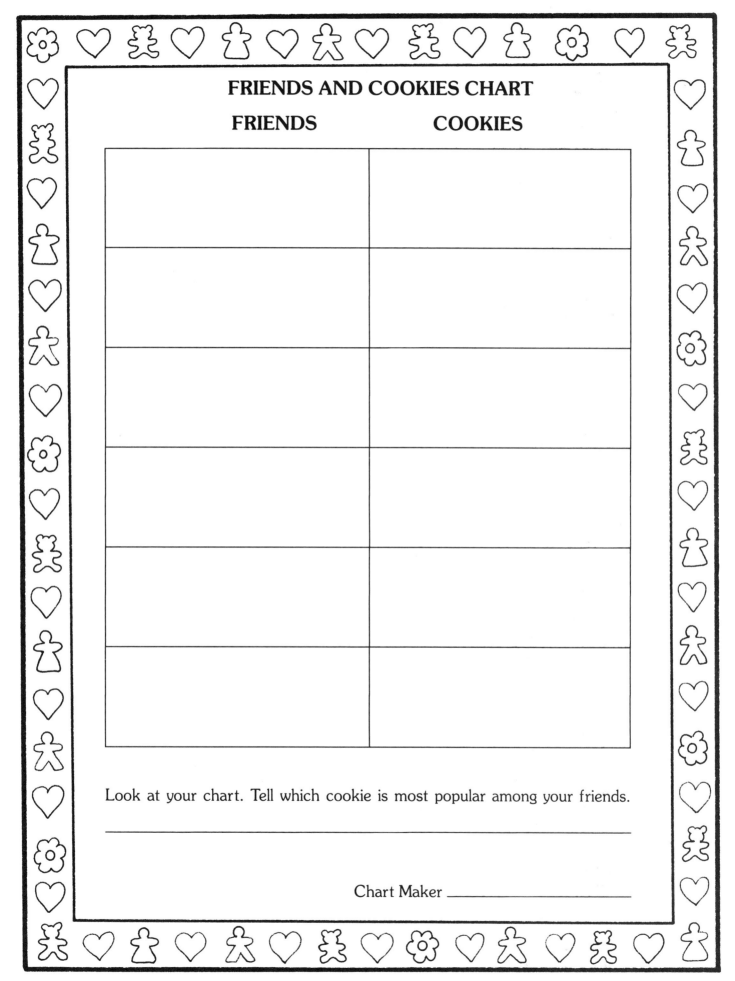

FRIENDS AND COOKIES CHART

FRIENDS	COOKIES

Look at your chart. Tell which cookie is most popular among your friends.

_____

Chart Maker _____

7

GA1164

Decorate Arthur's cookies so they are ready to hang on the Christmas tree.

Cookie Maker _____

GA1164

BEA AND MR. JONES

Amy Schwartz
Penguin Books, NY, 1983

A father and daughter trade places for the day. Bea joins the advertising world and Mr. Jones becomes a kindergartner.

BLOOM'S QUESTIONS

KNOWLEDGE
What did Bea and Mr. Jones do at the beginning of the story?

COMPREHENSION
Explain what Bea didn't like about kindergarten and what Mr. Jones didn't like about his advertising job.

APPLICATION
If you could trade places with someone, with whom would you trade? Why?

ANALYSIS
Compare how the teacher felt having Mr. Jones in class to how the executives felt having Bea in their company.

SYNTHESIS
What if Bea's father had been a construction worker, how would the story have been different?

EVALUATION
Judge how your teacher would react if your parent traded places with you.

CREATIVE THINKING ACTIVITIES

FLUENCY
Make a list of kindergarten activities.

FLEXIBILITY
Look at your list of kindergarten activities. Select which activity might be your parent's favorite. Tell why.

*ORIGINALITY
Make up a new verse to the Crumbly Cracker's jingle.
  "Munchy crunchy my dear snackers, you will love our Crumbly Crackers."

*ELABORATION
Help decorate Bea's office. Add as many details as you can. (Ask the principal to display these in the school office.)

GA1164

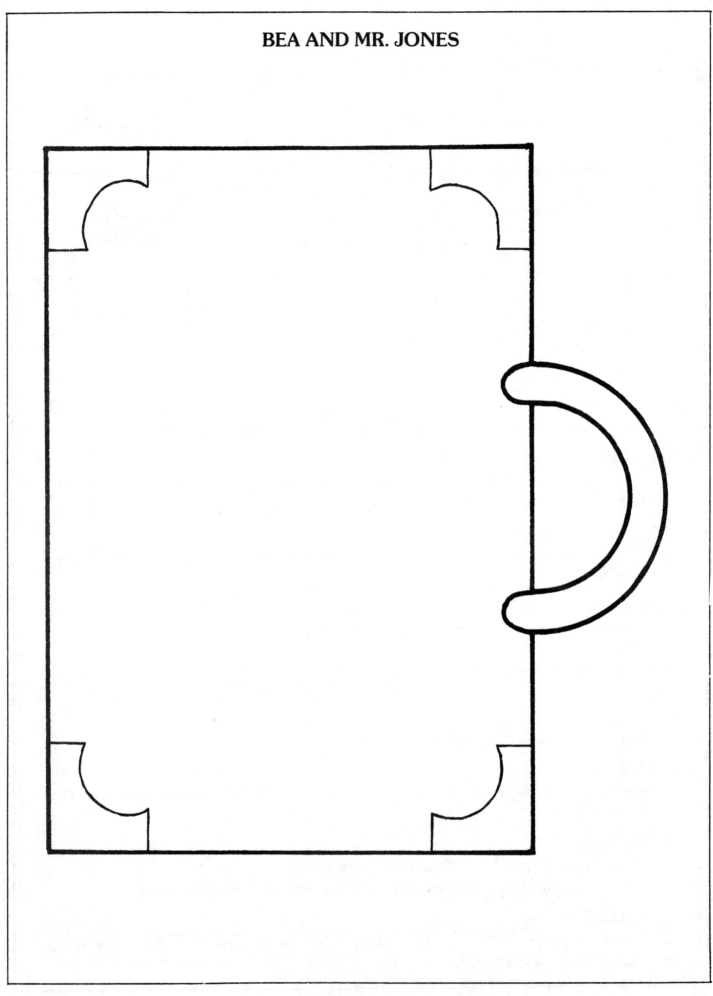

GA1164

Make up a new verse to the
Crumbly Cracker's jingle.

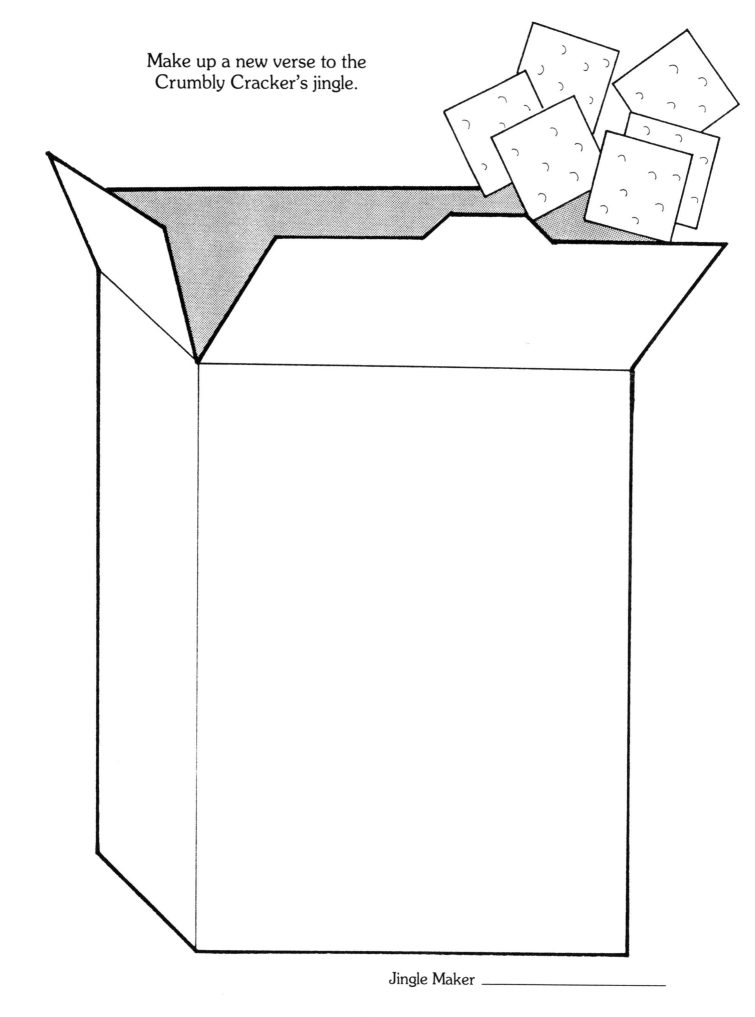

Jingle Maker _____

11

GA1164

Decorate Bea's office. Add as many details as you can.

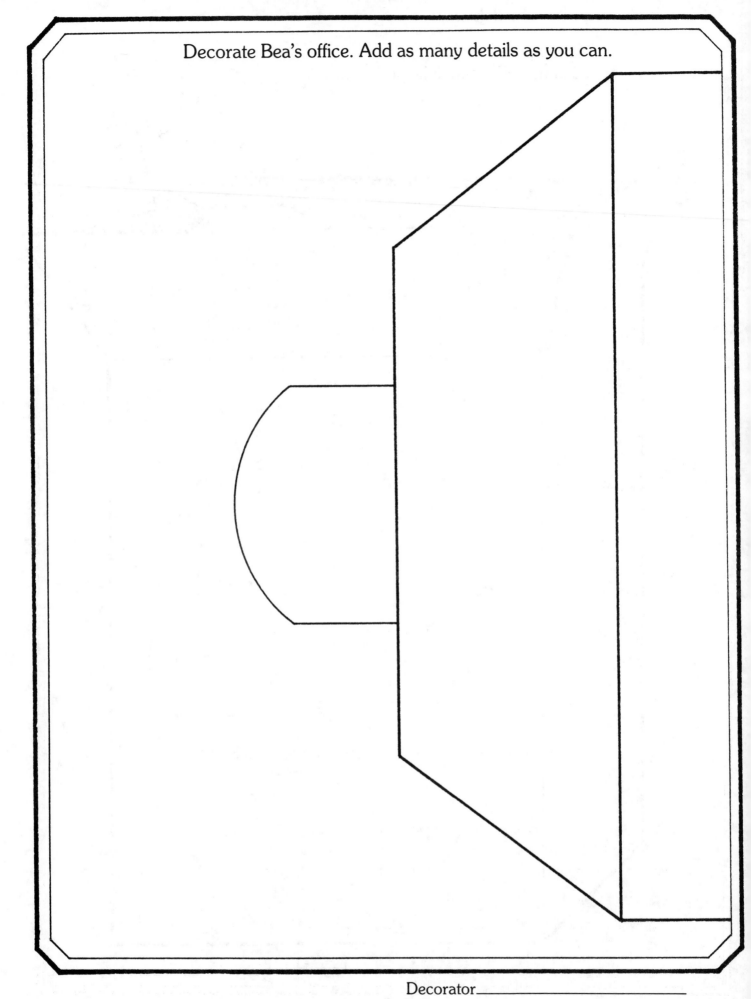

Decorator_____

12

BLUEBERRIES FOR SAL

Robert McCloskey
Scholastic, Inc., NY, 1976

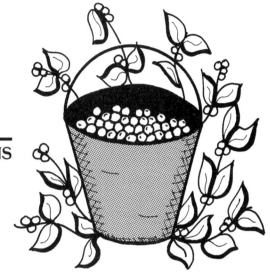

Little Sal and her mother encounter Mrs. Bear and her baby while picking blueberries on Blueberry Hill.

BLOOM'S QUESTIONS

KNOWLEDGE
What went "kuplink, kuplank, kuplunk"?

COMPREHENSION
Explain how Little Bear and Sal got mixed up.

APPLICATION
Sal's mother was going to can her blueberries. If you went blueberry picking, how would you use your blueberries?

ANALYSIS
How was Little Bear like little Sal?

SYNTHESIS
How would it have changed the story if Mama Bear hadn't been afraid of Sal?

EVALUATION
What evidence can you find in the story that demonstrates it is a fiction book?

CREATIVE THINKING ACTIVITIES

FLUENCY
Brainstorm a list of foods you can pick.

FLEXIBILITY
Categorize your list into foods that can be eaten raw and foods that require cooking before eating.

*ORIGINALITY
Create an original meal using blueberries. Make sure to name your creations. (You may want to have the students paste their menus inside construction paper folders. Have them decorate the fronts and invent restaurant names.)

*ELABORATION
Make a sign to place at the bottom of Blueberry Hill. Use mostly *B* words on your sign.

Create an original meal using blueberries. Make sure to name your creations.

Blueberry Menu

Chef _____

GA1164

Make a sign to place at the bottom of Blueberry Hill.
Use mostly *B* words on your sign.

Sign Maker_____

16

GA1164

A CHAIR FOR MY MOTHER

Vera B. Williams
Mulberry Books, NY, 1982

A family saves money for a comfortable, wonderful chair. The chair will replace the one that was destroyed in a terrible fire.

BLOOM'S QUESTIONS

KNOWLEDGE
Tell why Mama was saving money for a new chair.

COMPREHENSION
Explain how the family was saving money for the chair.

APPLICATION
If you were the little girl, what would you do to earn money for a chair?

ANALYSIS
Describe Mama's thoughts when she saw the fire engines in front of her house.

SYNTHESIS
Predict what the family will save for next. Invent a new way for them to save for it.

EVALUATION
Decide whether saving coins in a jar is a good way to save money.

CREATIVE THINKING ACTIVITIES

FLUENCY
Make a long list of all the places you might find a chair.

*FLEXIBILITY
Think of many uses for a chair. Draw your most unusual idea. (Assemble into a class book for all to enjoy.)

ORIGINALITY
Invent a chair you would like to have in your bedroom. Draw a picture of it. Tell what you would use it for.

*ELABORATION
Add details and personalize the money jar from the story.

GA1164

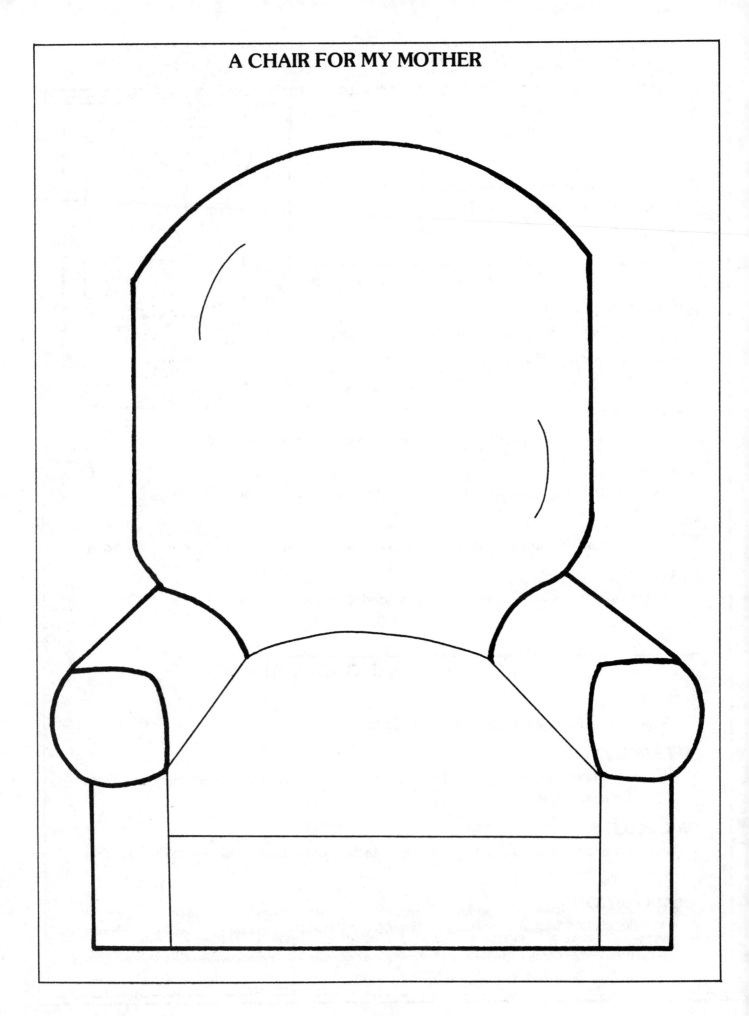

A CHAIR FOR MY MOTHER

GA1164

Draw your most unusual idea for the use of a chair.

Creative Thinker _____

19

GA1164

Add details and
personalize the
money jar.

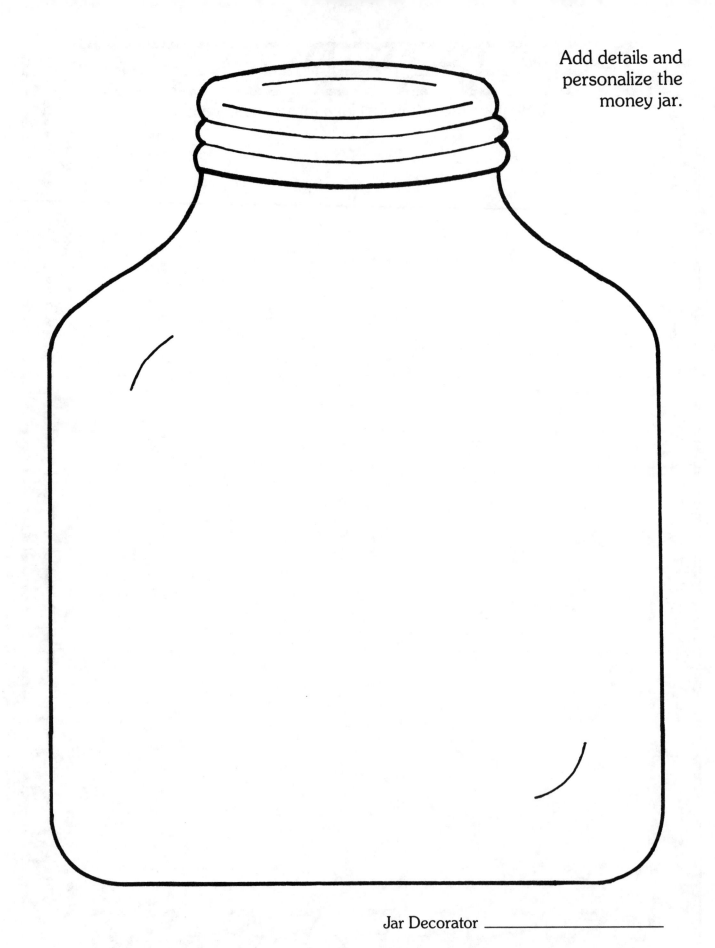

Jar Decorator _____

GOLDILOCKS AND THE THREE BEARS

Paul Galdone
Clarion Books, NY, 1972

Goldilocks wanders into the Three Bears' house. She tastes their porridge and tries out their chairs and beds. Goldilocks runs away when the bears return.

BLOOM'S QUESTIONS

KNOWLEDGE
What was the little girl's name?

COMPREHENSION
Why were there three bowls on the table?

APPLICATION
What do you do when your cereal is too hot?

ANALYSIS
List three differences between Papa Bear's cereal and Baby Bear's cereal.

SYNTHESIS
How would it have changed the story if the Three Bears had been home?

EVALUATION
Was Goldilocks smart to go into the Bears' house?

CREATIVE THINKING ACTIVITIES

FLUENCY
Make a long list of kinds of cereals.

FLEXIBILITY
Look at your list of cereals. Divide them into categories. How many categories did you create?

*ORIGINALITY
Invent a new kind of cereal for Bears. Design a box for your cereal. Include a name and a list of ingredients on your box. (Mount the completed cereal box on colored paper and display in the school lunchroom.)

*ELABORATION
Pretend Goldilocks found a plate and a cup next to each bowl of porridge. Draw a picture of what else the Three Bears are eating for breakfast.

GA1164

GOLDILOCKS AND THE THREE BEARS

GA1164

Design a box for a new kind of bear cereal.
Include a name and a list of ingredients.

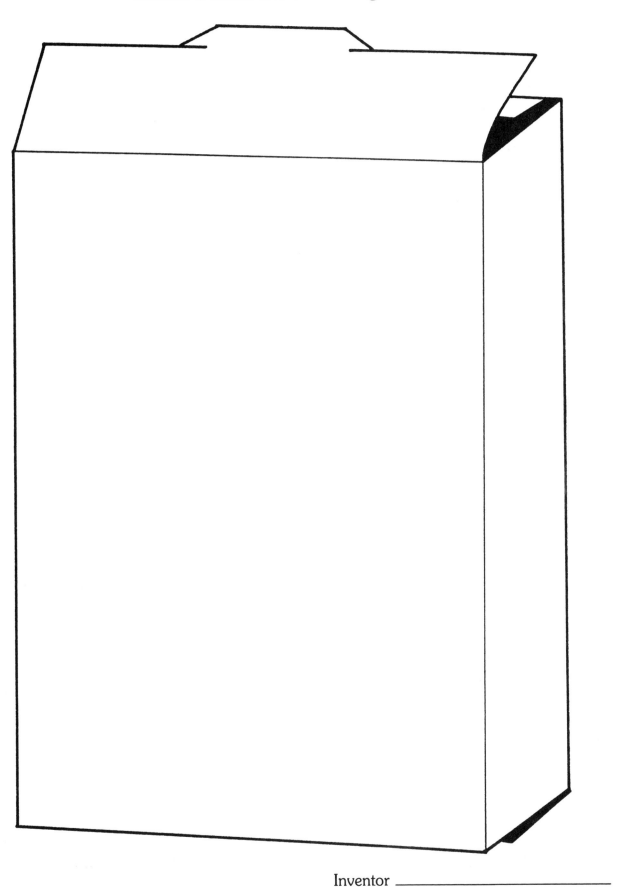

Inventor _____

Draw a picture of what else the Three Bears are eating for breakfast.

Menu Maker _____

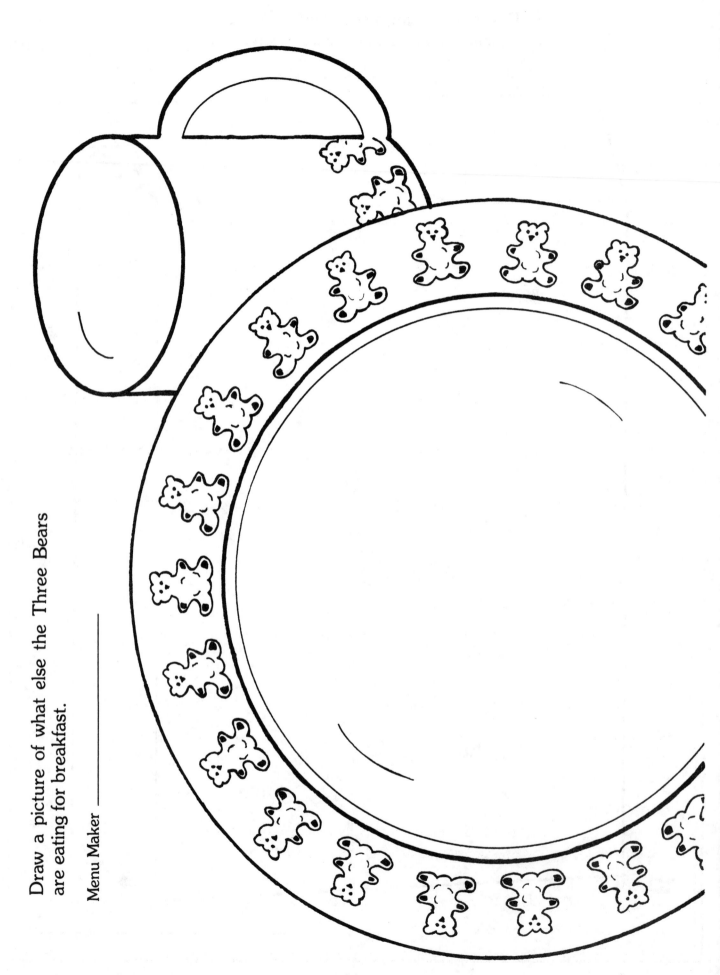

24

HECKEDY PEG

Audrey Wood
Harcourt Brace Jovanovich, NY, 1987

Seven children, a witch, and the children's mother form
a dramatic story based on a sixteenth century game.

BLOOM'S QUESTIONS

KNOWLEDGE
What were the two things the mother warned her children **not** to do?

COMPREHENSION
How did the witch get the children to disobey their mother?

APPLICATION
If you were the mother, what would you say to the witch to make her let you in?

ANALYSIS
Analyze the mother's thoughts when she came home and found her children missing.

SYNTHESIS
Choose seven children in your class to role-play a conversation in which Monday tries
to convince the other children **not** to let the witch in the house.

EVALUATION
Debate whether it's a good idea to talk to a stranger.

CREATIVE THINKING ACTIVITIES

FLUENCY
Make a long list of things that go together. (For example, cheese and crackers)

FLEXIBILITY
Draw a picture of your favorite idea from the above list. Compile your pictures into
a class book.

*ORIGINALITY
Make up a "Who Am I" riddle for one of the characters in the story. (Share the book
Heckedy Peg and your riddles with another classroom.)

*ELABORATION
Add details to Heckedy Peg's cane and turn it into something other than a cane. Label
your creation.

26

Choose one character from the story and create a "Who Am I"
riddle for it.

Riddler _____

_____

_____

_____

_____

_____

_____

_____

_____

Draw your character in the box. Then make a flap to hide your character.

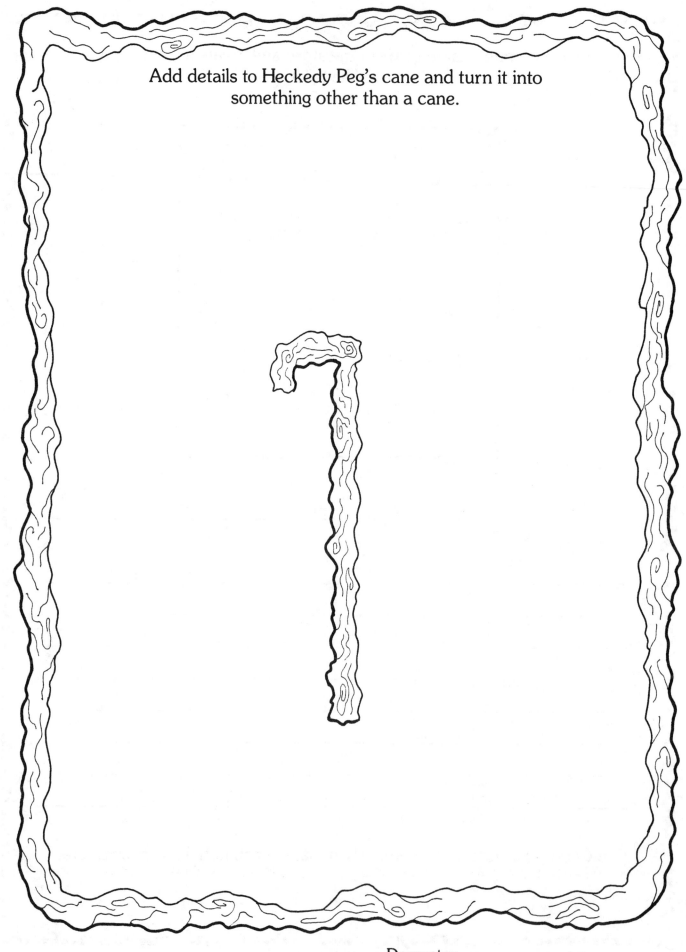

Add details to Heckedy Peg's cane and turn it into something other than a cane.

Decorator_____

28

IMOGENE'S ANTLERS

David Small
Crown Publishers, Inc., NY, 1985

Imogene wakes up one morning to discover that she has grown antlers during the night. Follow her adventure and family's reactions throughout the book.

BLOOM'S QUESTIONS

KNOWLEDGE
What was so unusual about Imogene?

COMPREHENSION
Describe how Imogene's mother tried to solve Imogene's problem.

APPLICATION
If you woke up with antlers, what is the first thing you would do?

ANALYSIS
Compare Imogene's day with that of a normal little girl.

SYNTHESIS
Create another way to hide Imogene's antlers.

EVALUATION
Judge which would be worse, having antlers or a peacock's tail.

CREATIVE THINKING ACTIVITIES

FLUENCY
Brainstorm a long list of uses for antlers.

*FLEXIBILITY
Draw a picture of your most unusual use of antlers.

*ORIGINALITY
Draw a picture of what Imogene will wake up looking like on Saturday. (If you have a classroom mirror, display the students' drawings around it.)

ELABORATION
Elaborate on the end of the story. What problems will Imogene encounter with a peacock's tail?

GA1164

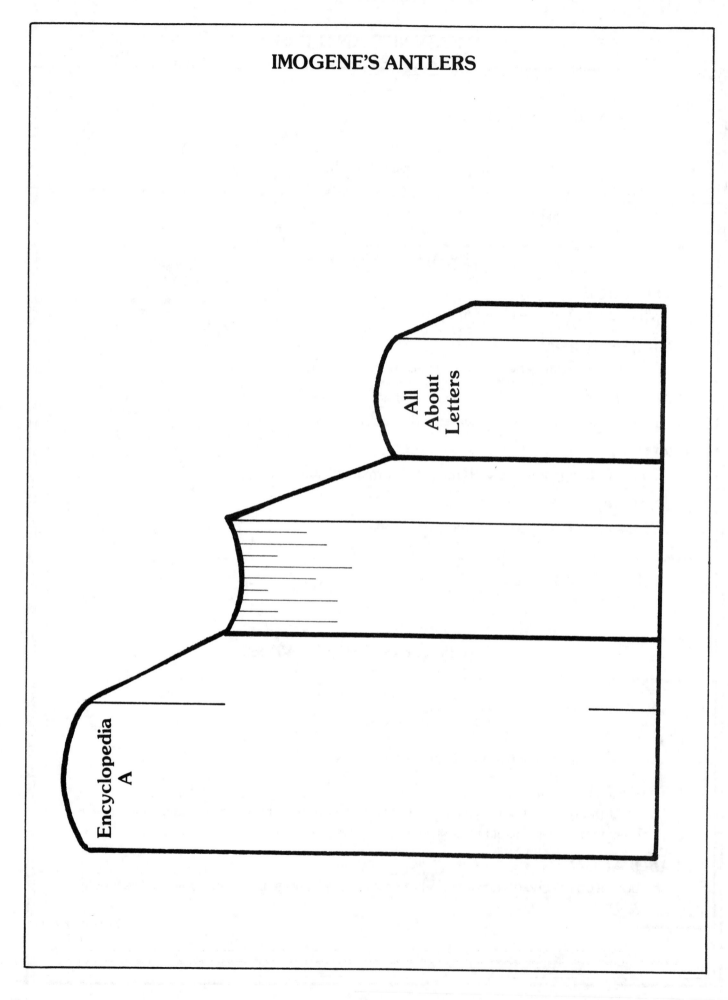

30

Draw a picture of an unusual use for Imogene's antlers.

Designer _____

31

What will Imogene look like when she wakes up on Saturday?

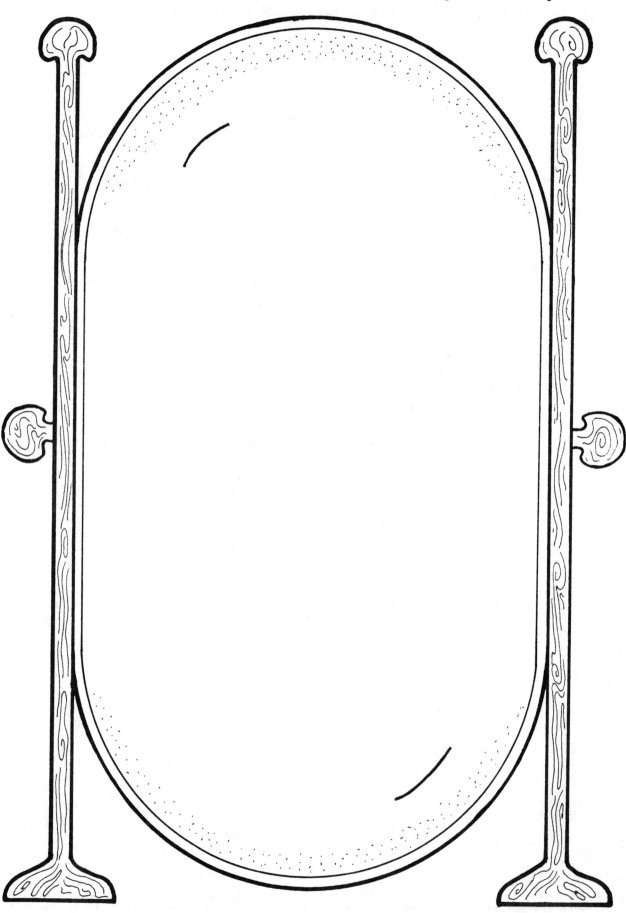

Fortune Teller _____

32

Bernard Waber
Scholastic, Inc., NY, 1972

Ira is going to his first sleepover at his friend Reggie's house. Ira has a hard time deciding whether or not to take his teddy bear.

BLOOM'S QUESTIONS

KNOWLEDGE
Tell what Ira wanted to take on his sleepover to Reggie's house.

COMPREHENSION
Explain why Ira finally went home to get his teddy bear.

*APPLICATION
Draw a picture of your favorite thing to sleep with.

ANALYSIS
How is sleeping at a friend's house different from sleeping at your own house?

SYNTHESIS
Predict what Ira would have done if Reggie had not had a bear, too.

EVALUATION
Decide how you feel about Ira's sister.

CREATIVE THINKING ACTIVITIES

FLUENCY
Make a long list of kinds or names of bears.

FLEXIBILITY
Think of something else Ira might like to sleep with.

ORIGINALITY
Create a My "Beary" Special Thing Day at school. Bring your favorite thing to sleep with. Share why it is special with your class.

*ELABORATION
Add the finishing details to a wardrobe for Tah Tah. (Display the completed teddy bears in the library. Label the display A Teddy Bear Fashion Show.)

GA1164

IRA SLEEPS OVER

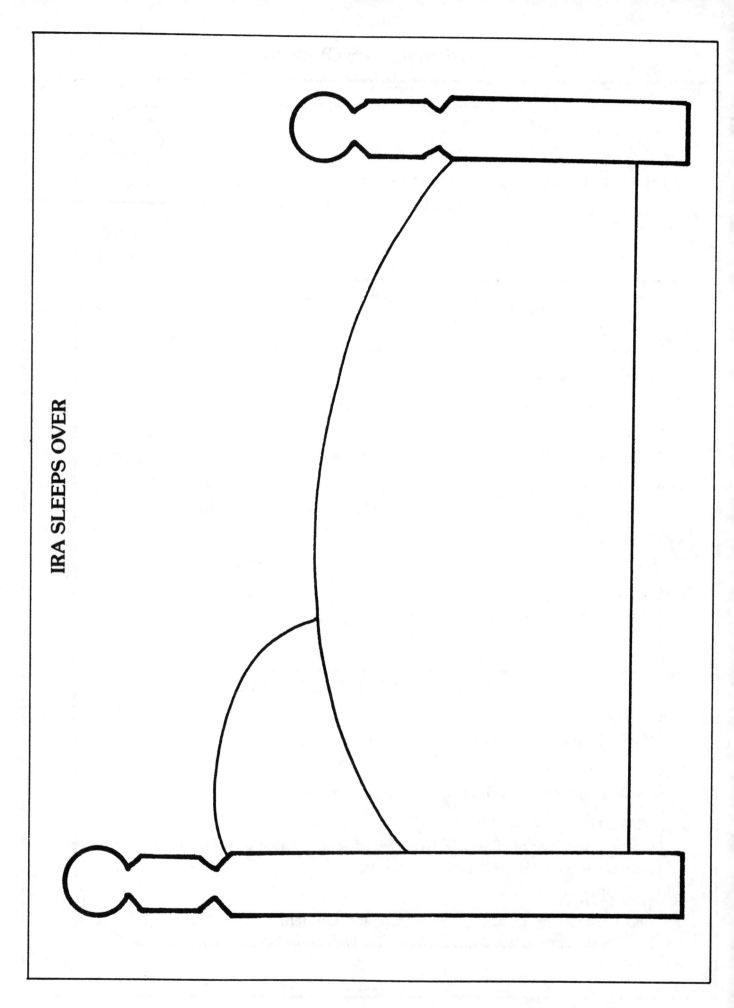

34

Draw a picture of your favorite
thing to sleep with.

Snuggler _____

35

Color and cut out the Tah Tah paper doll.

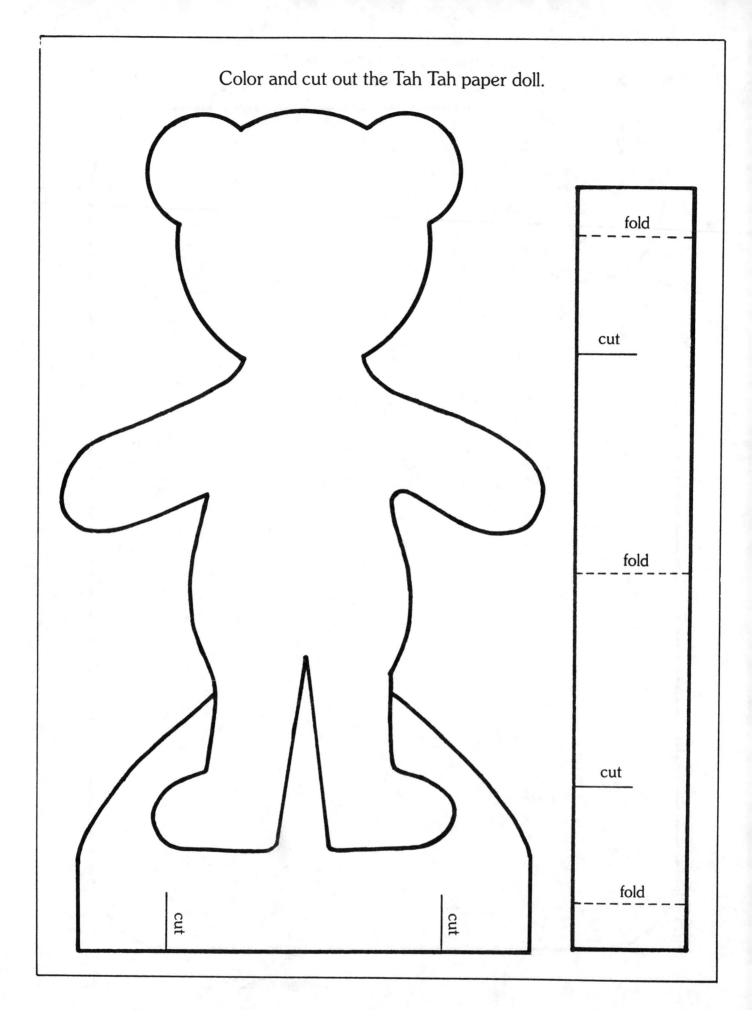

GA1164

Add the finishing details to Tah Tah's wardrobe.

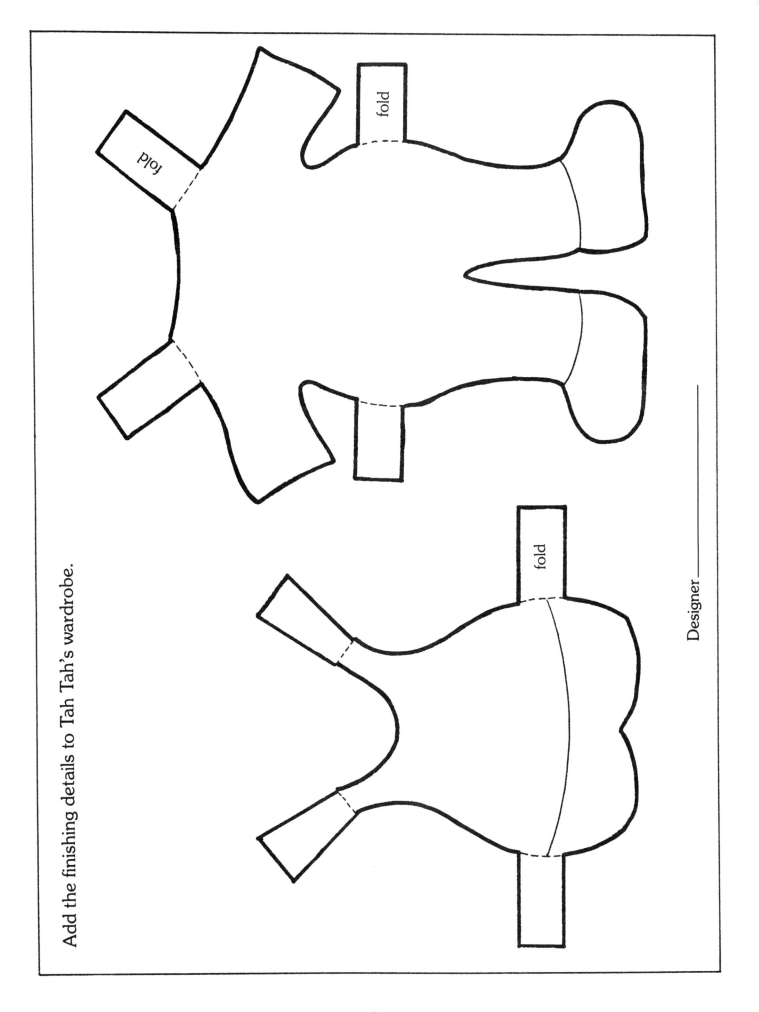

fold

fold

fold

fold

Designer _____

37

Use these circles to create an accessory for each bear outfit.

38

JUMANJI

Chris Van Allsburg
Houghton Mifflin Co., Boston, MA, 1981

Peter and Judy are left alone and discover the game
and adventures of Jumanji.

BLOOM'S QUESTIONS

KNOWLEDGE
Name the imaginary adventures Peter and Judy encountered while playing the game.

COMPREHENSION
Why did the adults laugh when Peter began to tell them about the adventures?

APPLICATION
Which adventure would you **least** like to encounter?

ANALYSIS
Compare the game of Jumanji to the game of Candy Land.

SYNTHESIS
Predict what will happen to Danny and Walter Budwig.

EVALUATION
Decide if it was a good idea for Paul and Judy to return the game to the park. Why
or why not?

CREATIVE THINKING ACTIVITIES

FLUENCY
Make a long list of board games.

FLEXIBILITY
Think of other times or situations when you might **want** to play Jumanji.

*ORIGINALITY
Leave a note on the game box for the next Jumanji player.

*ELABORATION
Create one more adventure in the game of Jumanji. Draw a picture of it on the game
square.

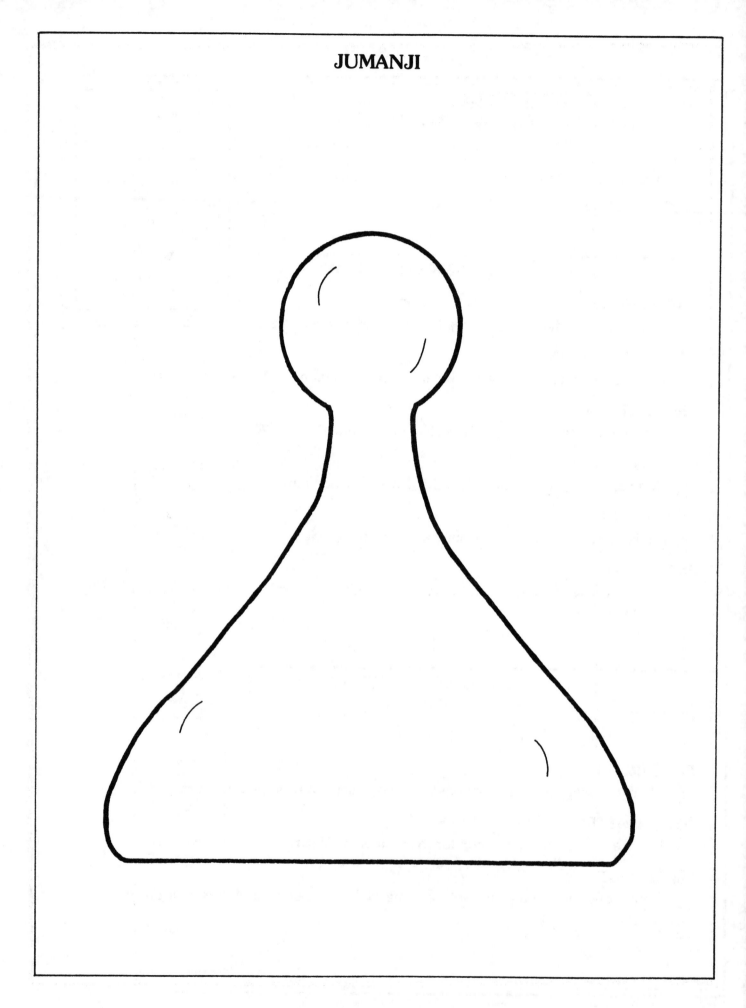

40

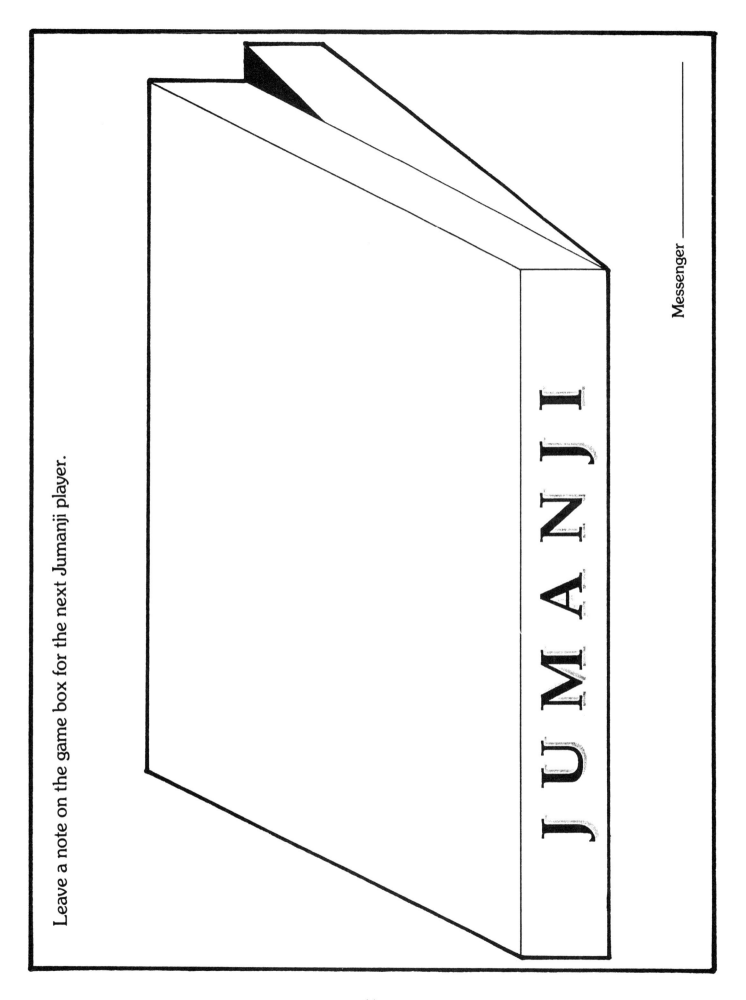

Leave a note on the game box for the next Jumanji player.

Messenger _____

JUMANJI

41

Create one more adventure in the game of Jumanji.
Draw a picture of it on the game square.

Game Maker _____

START

GA1164

MILLIONS OF CATS

Wanda Gag
Coward-McCann, Inc., 1956

"Hundreds of cats, thousands of cats, millions and billions and trillions of cats" share the pages of this beloved tale.

BLOOM'S QUESTIONS

KNOWLEDGE
Where did the old man find the cats?

COMPREHENSION
Explain how all the cats disappeared.

APPLICATION
The old man had difficulty deciding which cat he liked the best. Share a time when you had difficulty making a decision.

ANALYSIS
Tell which parts of the story could really happen and which parts are make-believe.

*SYNTHESIS
Describe an imaginary cat in detail to a partner. Have your partner try to draw it as you explain it. (Decorate a school window with cat paw prints and display students' drawings around them.)

EVALUATION
What other methods could the cats have used to solve the problem of who was going to live with the old man and woman?

CREATIVE THINKING ACTIVITIES

FLUENCY
Brainstorm as many different kinds of cats as you can.

FLEXIBILITY
Write five or more words to describe one of the cats on your list.

*ORIGINALITY
Design wrapping paper using a cat pattern.

ELABORATION
The old woman and the old man provided their cat with a ball of yarn and a bowl. Using the back of your wrapping paper, draw a picture of another gift appropriate for a cat.

GA1164

44

Describe an imaginary cat in detail to a partner. Have your partner draw it as you explain it.

Cat Visualizer _____

45

GA1164

Design wrapping paper using a cat pattern.

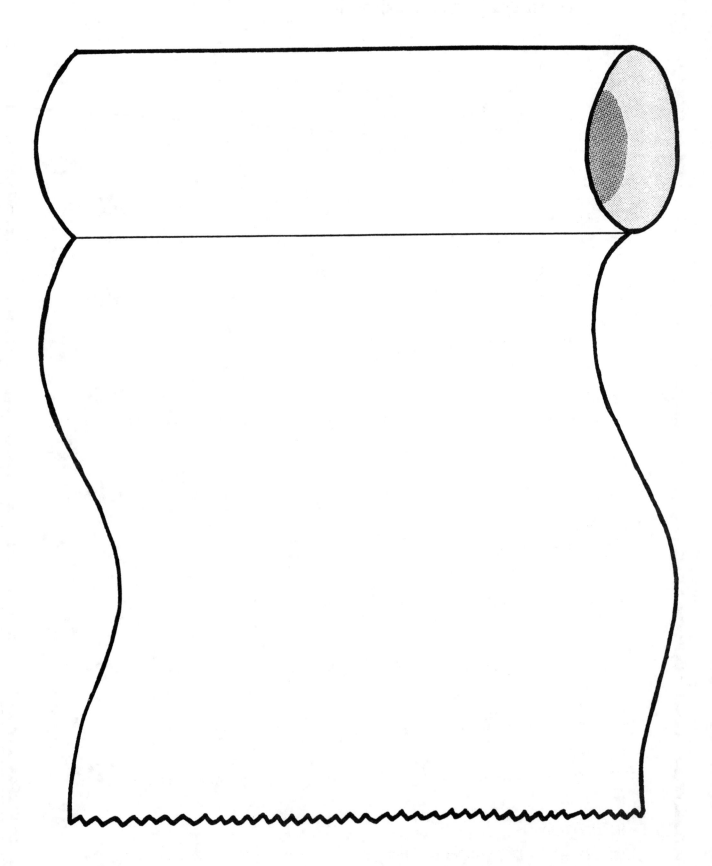

Paper Maker _____

46

MING LO MOVES THE MOUNTAIN

Arnold Lobel
Greenwillow Books, NY, 1982

The tale of Ming Lo and his wife's desire to move the mountain is shared in this tale of rural China.

BLOOM'S QUESTIONS

KNOWLEDGE
Who are the main characters in the story?

COMPREHENSION
Why did Ming Lo follow the wise man's advice?

APPLICATION
If you wanted to change something about the place where you lived, what would it be? How would you change it?

ANALYSIS
Gather evidence from the story indicating that Ming Lo and his wife were not very wise.

SYNTHESIS
Create another dance for Ming Lo and his wife to follow that would "move the mountain."

EVALUATION
Judge whether the wise man was really wise.

CREATIVE THINKING ACTIVITIES

FLUENCY
Brainstorm a list of things that are "impossible" to move.

FLEXIBILITY
Select and "impossible thing" from your list and devise a plan to move it.

*ORIGINALITY
Elaborate on the contents of Ming Lo's bundle. Make his most valuable possession the largest.

*ELABORATION
Help Ming Low reassemble this bundle of sticks into something else he might need.

GA1164

Elaborate on the contents of Ming Lo's bundle.
Make his most valuable possession the largest.

Wise Person_____

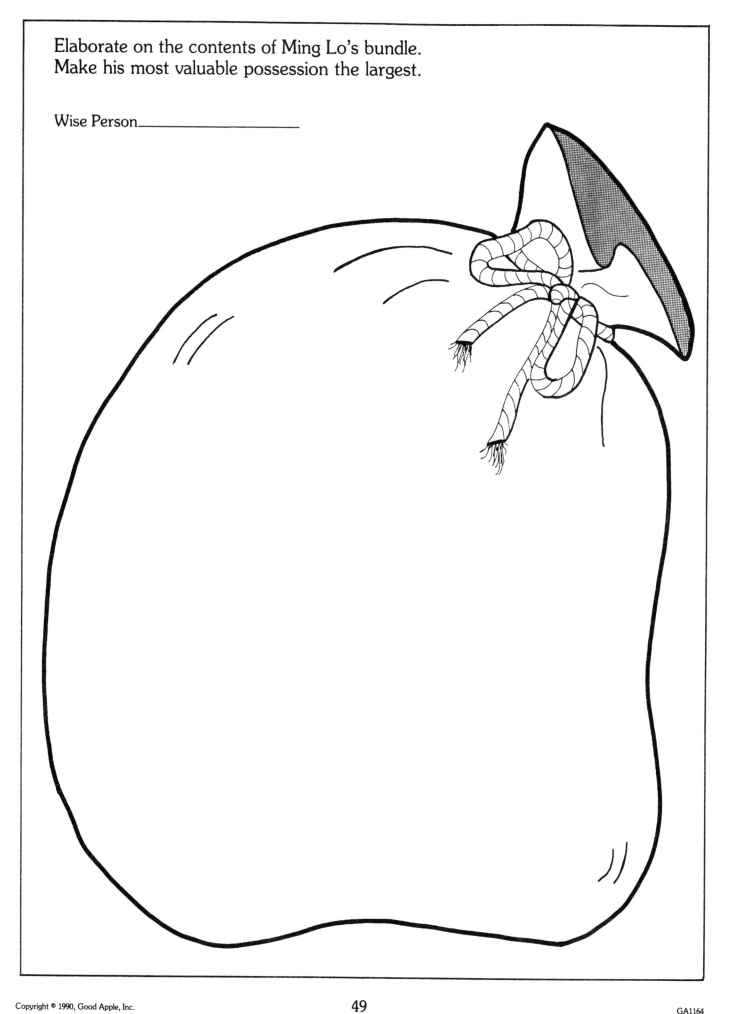

49

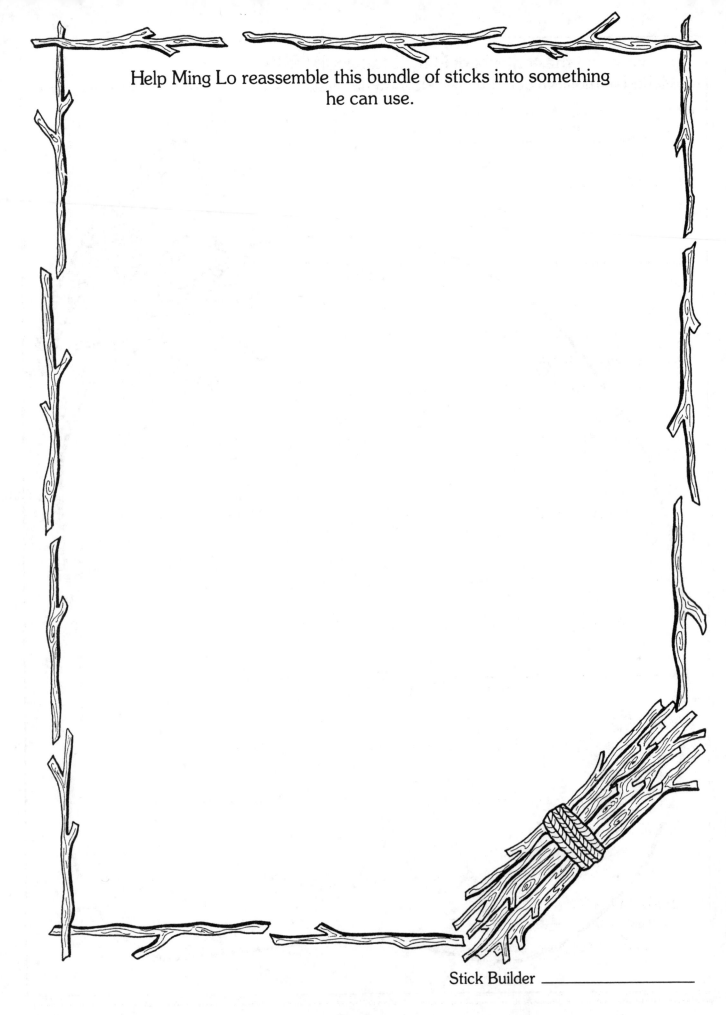

Help Ming Lo reassemble this bundle of sticks into something he can use.

Stick Builder _____

GA1164

MISS NELSON IS MISSING

Harry Allard and James Marshall
Scholastic, Inc., NY, 1977

Miss Nelson disappears from her unruly class. A stranger appears ready to make the students behave.

BLOOM'S QUESTIONS

KNOWLEDGE
Which character is the focus of this story?

COMPREHENSION
Describe in detail the setting of the story.

APPLICATION
Pretend you are a student in Miss Nelson's classroom. Write five things you would feel when you meet Miss Viola Swamp.

ANALYSIS
Compare Viola Swamp to Miss Nelson. How are they alike? How are they different?

SYNTHESIS
Imagine what might have happened if Viola Swamp had been a sweet old lady?

EVALUATION
Was Miss Nelson's trick a good one? Why or why not?

CREATIVE THINKING ACTIVITIES

FLUENCY
Make a long list of all the school things that come to your mind.

FLEXIBILITY
Think of other ways Miss Nelson could use her Viola Swamp costume.

*ORIGINALITY
Design a new disguise for Miss Nelson. (This activity would make a great bulletin board during Halloween. Title the bulletin board "A New Disguise for Miss Nelson.")

*ELABORATION
The children think of three unlikely things that may have happened to Miss Nelson. Illustrate your own unlikely suggestion for Miss Nelson's disappearance.

GA1164

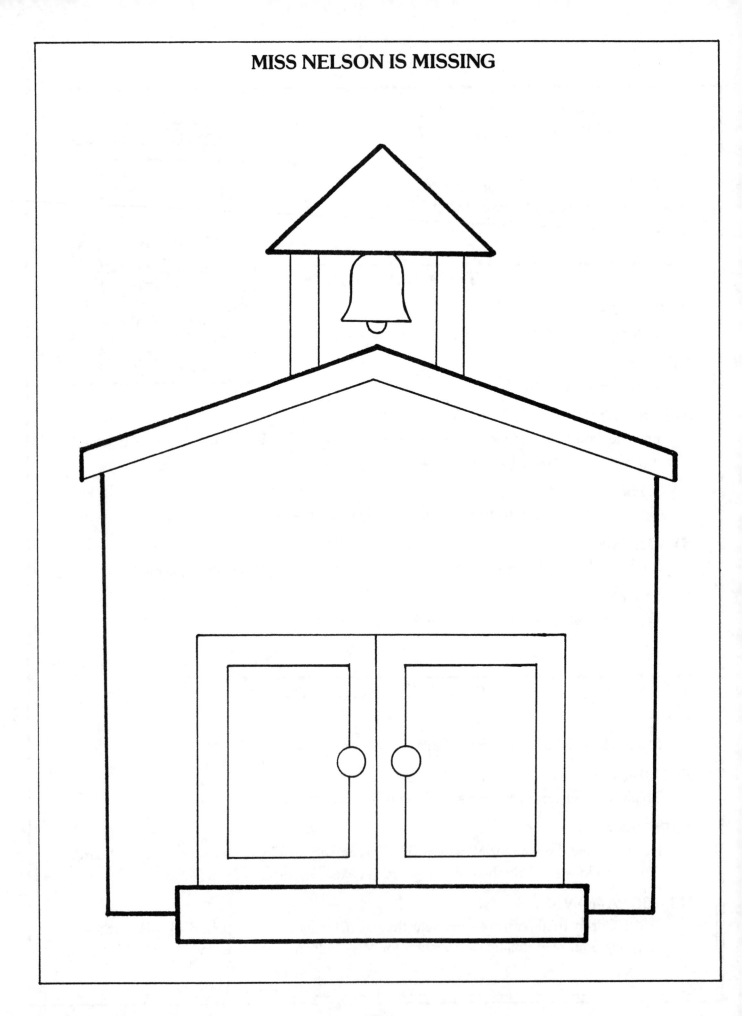

MISS NELSON IS MISSING

GA1164

Illustrate your own unlikely suggestion for Miss Nelson's disappearance.

Costume Designer _____

53

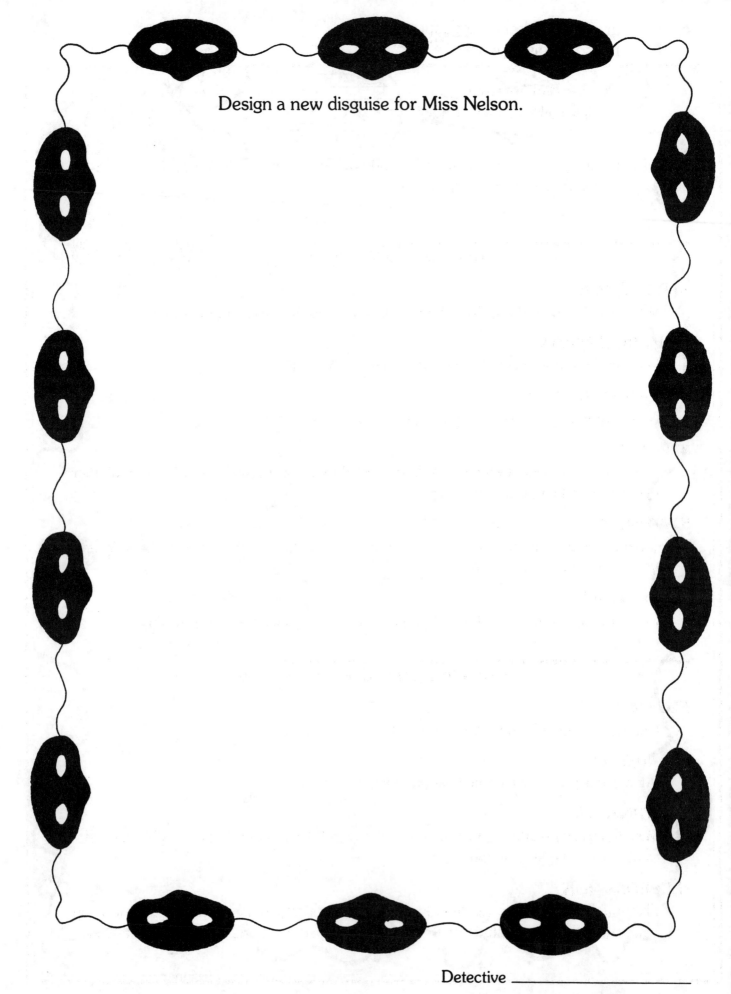

Design a new disguise for Miss Nelson.

Detective _____

54

MISS RUMPHIUS

Barbara Cooney
Viking Penguin, Inc., 1982

Alice Rumphius is "told" to make the world more beautiful. This story tells how she did it.

BLOOM'S QUESTIONS

KNOWLEDGE

What are the three things Miss Rumphius wanted to do like her grandfather?

COMPREHENSION

How did Miss Rumphius get her name, The Lupine Lady?

APPLICATION

Name three things you want to be sure to do in your lifetime.

ANALYSIS

Compare how Miss Rumphius made the world more beautiful, to how her grandfather made it more beautiful.

SYNTHESIS

Suppose Miss Rumphius had been confined to bed forever, how could she still have made her wonderful idea come true?

EVALUATION

Evaluate the importance of Miss Rumphius' and her grandfather's storytelling.

CREATIVE THINKING ACTIVITIES

FLUENCY

Brainstorm beautiful things in the world.

FLEXIBILITY

Rank order your five favorite beautiful things.

*ORIGINALITY

Miss Rumphius made a contribution to the world. What contribution could you make to the world? Draw it on the easel.

*ELABORATION

Elaborate on this apron for Miss Rumphius to wear. Make sure it has a place to keep her seeds. (Encourage students to use colored paper, yarn, and/or other art materials.)

GA1164

Draw your contribution to the world on the easel.

Beautifier _____

57

GA1164

Elaborate on this apron for Miss Rumphius to wear.
Make sure it has a place to keep her seeds.

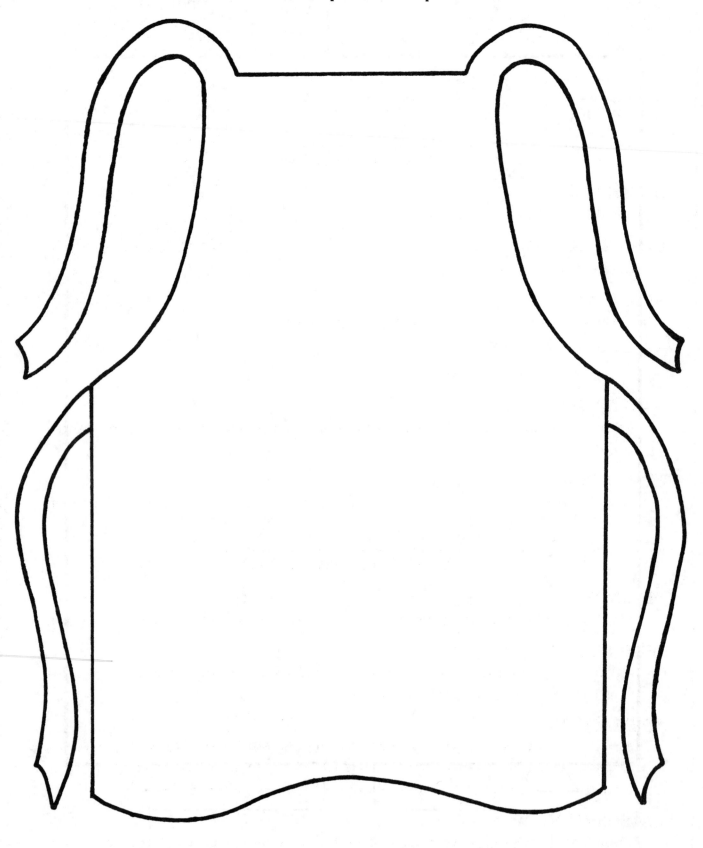

Handicrafter _____

58

MOVING MOLLY

Shirley Hughes
Prentice-Hall, Inc., NJ, 1979

A family moves from an apartment to a house with a yard and experiences the sadness and joy of moving.

BLOOM'S QUESTIONS

KNOWLEDGE
List the ways Molly spent her day in the city.

COMPREHENSION
Explain why Molly's family moved.

APPLICATION
If you were Molly, how would you have felt about your new house?

ANALYSIS
Compare Molly's new house with her old house.

SYNTHESIS
Imagine the twins had not moved next door to Molly. How would it have changed the story?

EVALUATION
Was it a good idea for Molly to go through the hole in the fence? Explain your answer.

CREATIVE THINKING ACTIVITIES

FLUENCY
Make a list of questions you would ask your parents if you found out you were moving.

*FLEXIBILITY
Molly's brother and sister made a go-cart from Molly's old baby carriage. What other uses can you think of for a baby carriage?

*ORIGINALITY
Molly's mom was busy wallpapering and painting the new house. Design three samples of wallpaper for Molly's new house. Tell in what rooms they will be used. (A fun idea: wallpaper a corner of your classroom with students' original samples.)

ELABORATION
Moving Molly is an example of alliteration. Elaborate on the names of your classmates by using alliteration. For example: Exciting Ellen, Lovely Laurie, Fabulous Frank, and Daring Dave.

GA1164

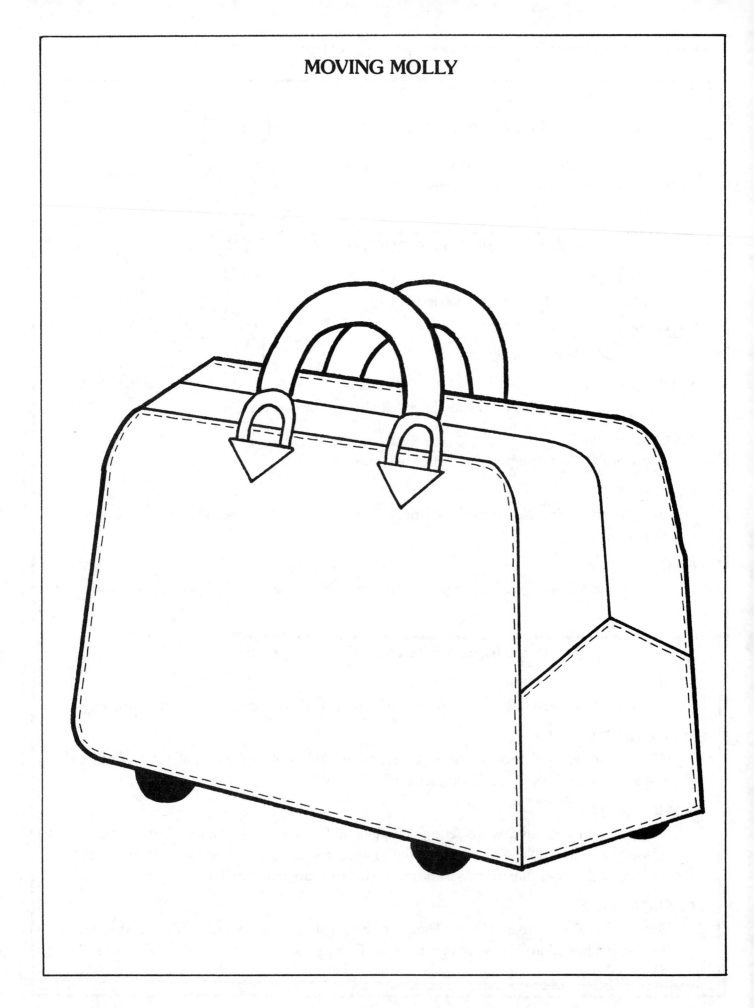

GA1164

Invent a new use for this baby carriage.

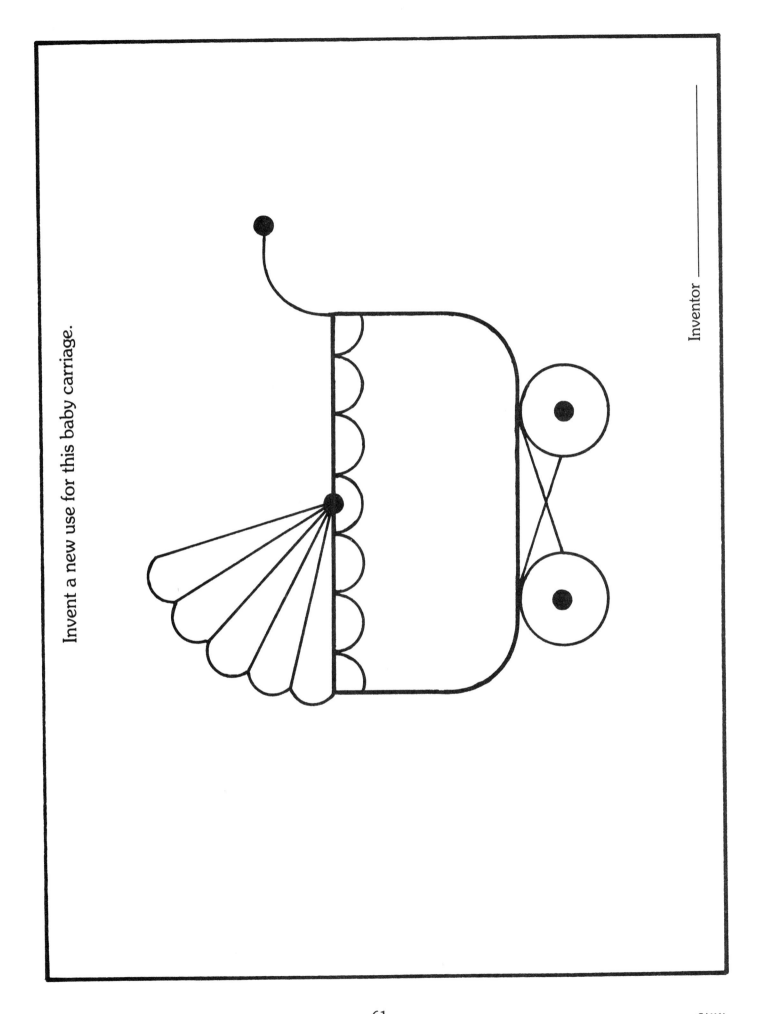

Inventor _____

GA1164

Design three samples of wallpaper for Molly's new house.
Tell in what rooms they will be used.

Decorator _____

62

GA1164

THE ONE IN THE MIDDLE IS THE GREEN KANGAROO

Judy Blume
Dell Publishing Co., NY, 1981

Freddy has a left-out kind of feeling because he is the middle child. The story explores his chance to show everyone how special he is.

BLOOM'S QUESTIONS

KNOWLEDGE
Describe the members of the play's cast.

COMPREHENSION
Tell what Freddy had to do to get the part of the green kangaroo.

APPLICATION
If you were Freddy, how would you have spoken the line, "I'm the green kangaroo!"? How would you have jumped as the green kangaroo?

ANALYSIS
Analyze what would have happened if Freddy went to change into his kangaroo costume on the day of the play and found it missing.

SYNTHESIS
Write a tongue twister about a kangaroo.

EVALUATION
Discuss the pros and cons of being a middle child. Decide whether you think it's a good or bad position to hold in a family.

CREATIVE THINKING ACTIVITIES

FLUENCY
Freddy is the middle child in his family. Brainstorm all the things you know that are in the middle.

FLEXIBILITY
Freddy's green kangaroo costume was perfect for the play. What else could you do with a green kangaroo costume?

*ORIGINALITY
Conduct an interview with your sibling.

*ELABORATION
Freddy wished he was not in the middle. Write three other wishes Freddy might have wished.

GA1164

**THE ONE IN THE MIDDLE IS
THE GREEN KANGAROO**

64

Freddy's Book of Wishes

Write three other wishes Freddy might have dreamed about. Cut out the wishes and staple them into a wish book.

Wishful Thinker _____

GA1164

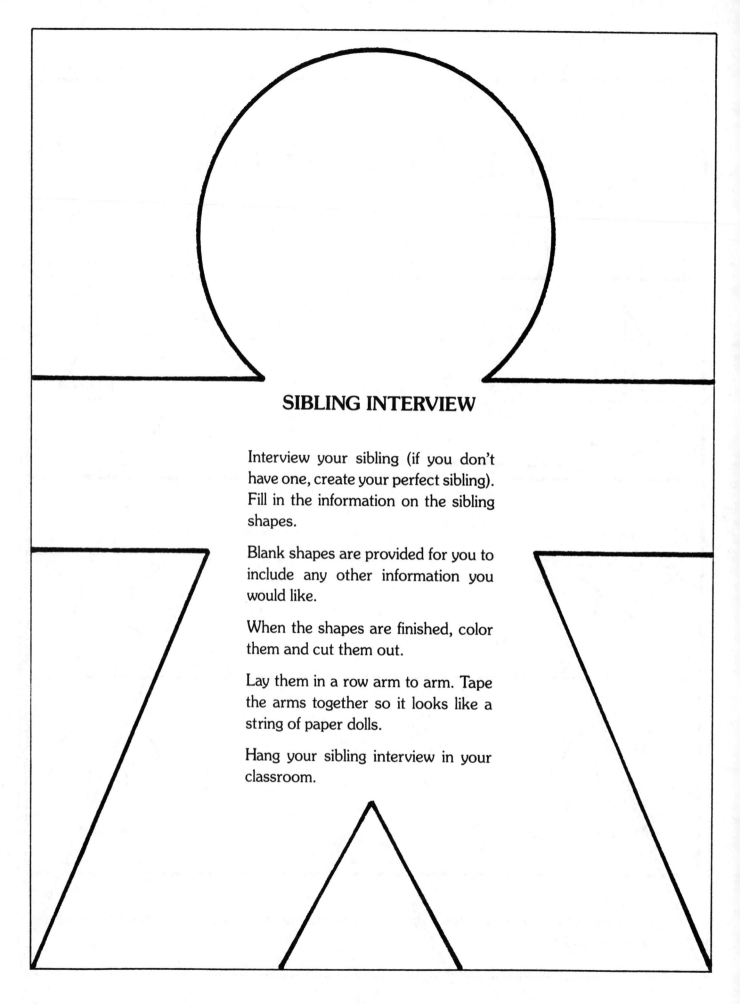

SIBLING INTERVIEW

Interview your sibling (if you don't have one, create your perfect sibling). Fill in the information on the sibling shapes.

Blank shapes are provided for you to include any other information you would like.

When the shapes are finished, color them and cut them out.

Lay them in a row arm to arm. Tape the arms together so it looks like a string of paper dolls.

Hang your sibling interview in your classroom.

GA1164

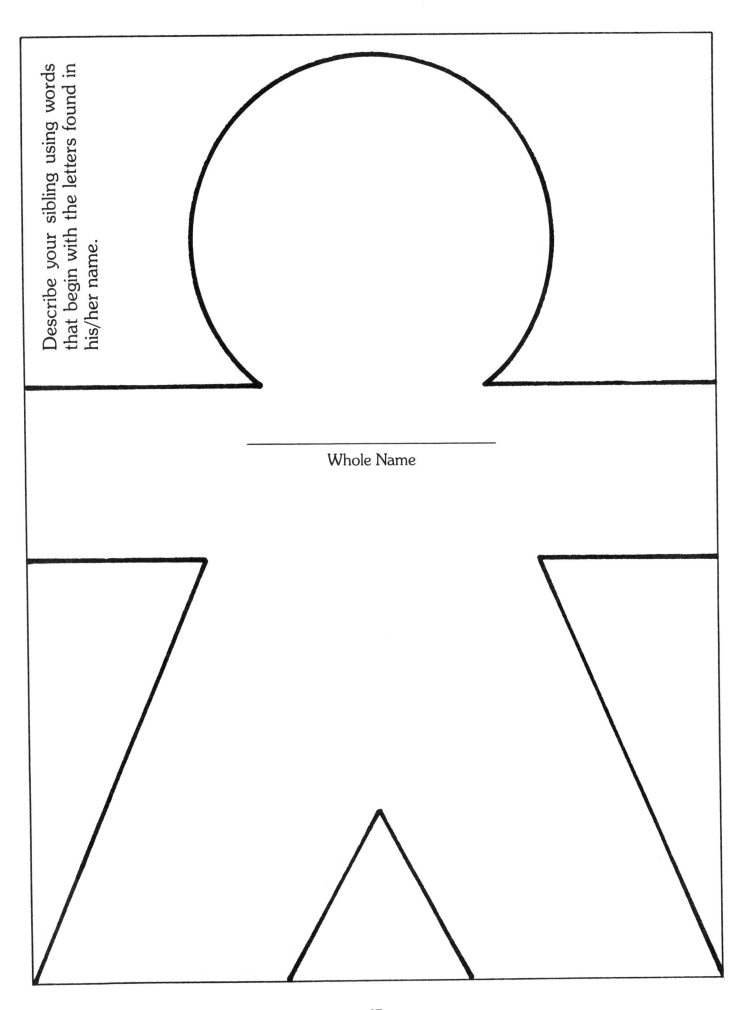

Describe your sibling using words that begin with the letters found in his/her name.

_____

Whole Name

GA1164

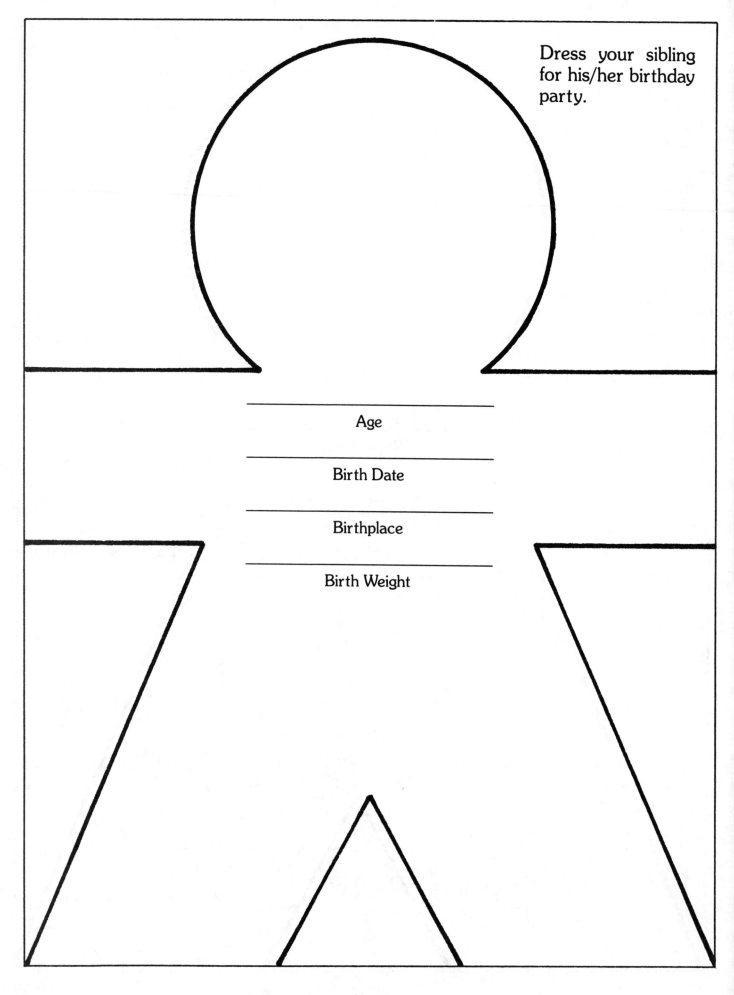

Dress your sibling for his/her birthday party.

Age

Birth Date

Birthplace

Birth Weight

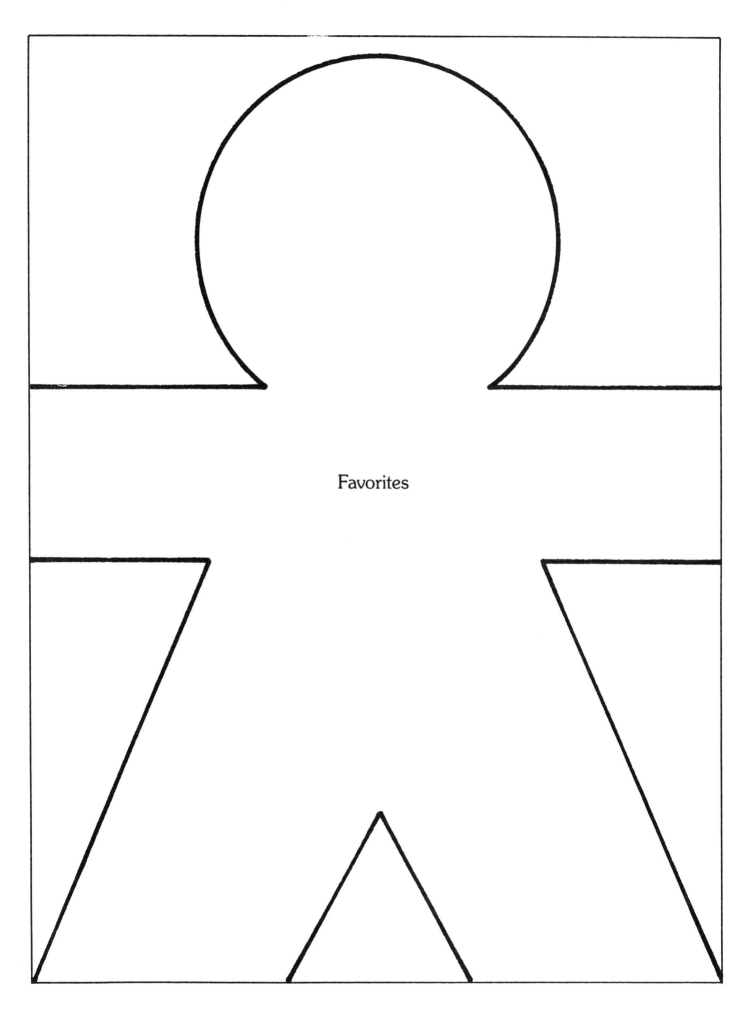

Favorites

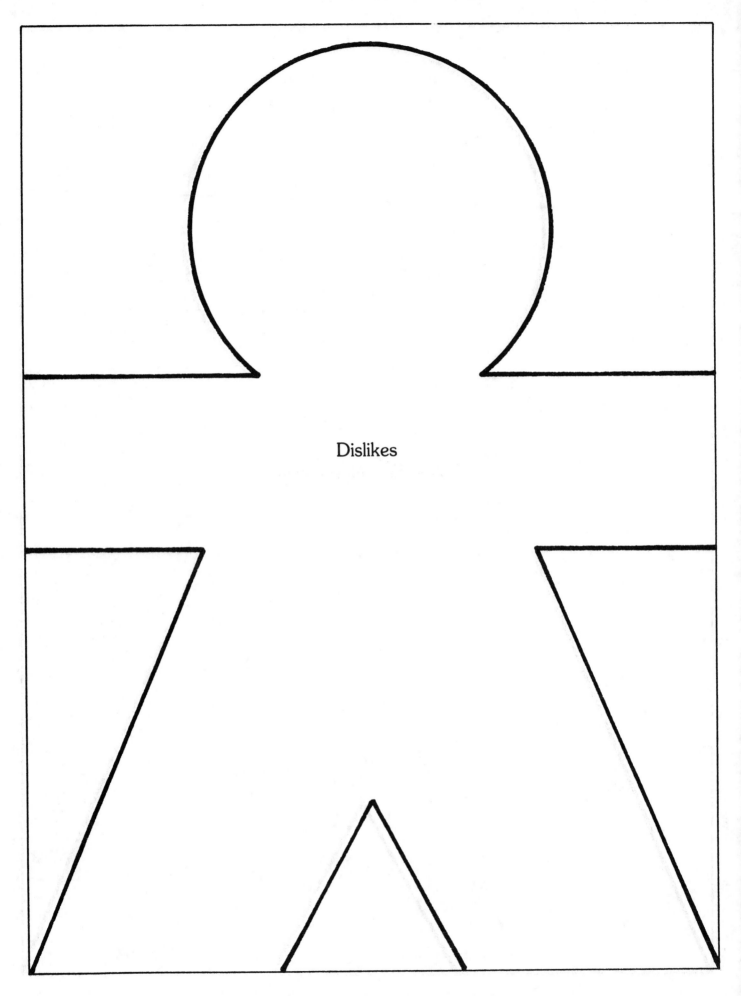

Dislikes

70

Things We Do Together

71

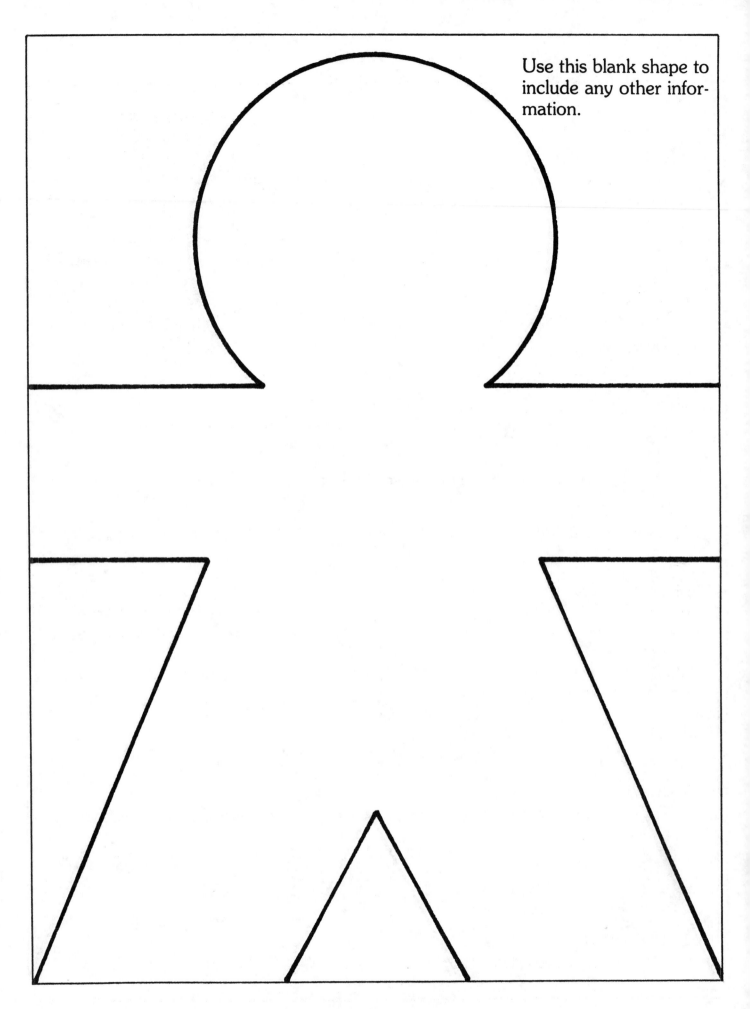

Use this blank shape to include any other information.

GA1164

OWL MOON

Jane Yolen
The Putnam Publishing Group, NY, 1987

A young girl and her father share a special walk together while going owling on a snowy, moonlit night.

BLOOM'S QUESTIONS

KNOWLEDGE
What is the setting of the story?

COMPREHENSION
Why do you have to be brave and quiet when you go owling?

APPLICATION
Tell about something you have waited a long time to be old enough to do.

ANALYSIS
Compare owling to other nighttime activities.

*SYNTHESIS
If you could talk to the owl, what four questions would you ask him? (Exchange students' papers. Have students pretend they are the owl and answer the questions given them.)

EVALUATION
The little girl was not disappointed when her father called the first time and the owl did not come. Do you think she would have been disappointed if the owl had not come at all that night? Why or why not?

CREATIVE THINKING ACTIVITIES

FLUENCY
List other activities or places where patience is required.

FLEXIBILITY
Look at your list above. Which situation would require the most patience from you? Why?

*ORIGINALITY
The little girl and her father left gray tracks in the snow. Think of other things that leave tracks. Illustrate one of them.

ELABORATION
Through discussion, elaborate on the meaning of the text on the last page of the story.

GA1164

OWL MOON

If you could talk to the owl, what four questions
would you ask him?

Owl Interviewer_____

Draw some tracks in the snow.
Make them lead to the box. Put a flap over
the box. Can your friends guess what's
hiding behind the flap?

Track Maker _____

76

THE PAIN AND THE GREAT ONE

Judy Blume
Dell Publishing Co., NY, 1974

A brother/sister relationship is explained through a series of humorous incidents, each sibling wondering who is loved more.

BLOOM'S QUESTIONS

KNOWLEDGE

Who is "The Pain"? Who is "The Great One"?

COMPREHENSION

Give three reasons why The Great One thinks The Pain should go to bed earlier.

APPLICATION

If someone ruined your city made from blocks, how would you feel and what would you say to him?

ANALYSIS

Compare The Great One's story to The Pain's story. How are they alike? How are they different?

SYNTHESIS

Pretend you are the mother. How would you have handled the relationship between The Great One and The Pain?

EVALUATION

Decide how The Pain and The Great One really feel about each other. Explain your answer using *evidence* from the story.

CREATIVE THINKING ACTIVITIES

FLUENCY

Write a list of things that "bug" you.

FLEXIBILITY

The Great One watches Aunt Diana's baby sleeping in the dresser drawer. What are some other uses for a dresser drawer?

*ORIGINALITY

Design a building block creation that someone in your family can use.

*ELABORATION

The Pain and The Great One are playing and they have found something they enjoy doing together. Draw a picture of what they are doing.

GA1164

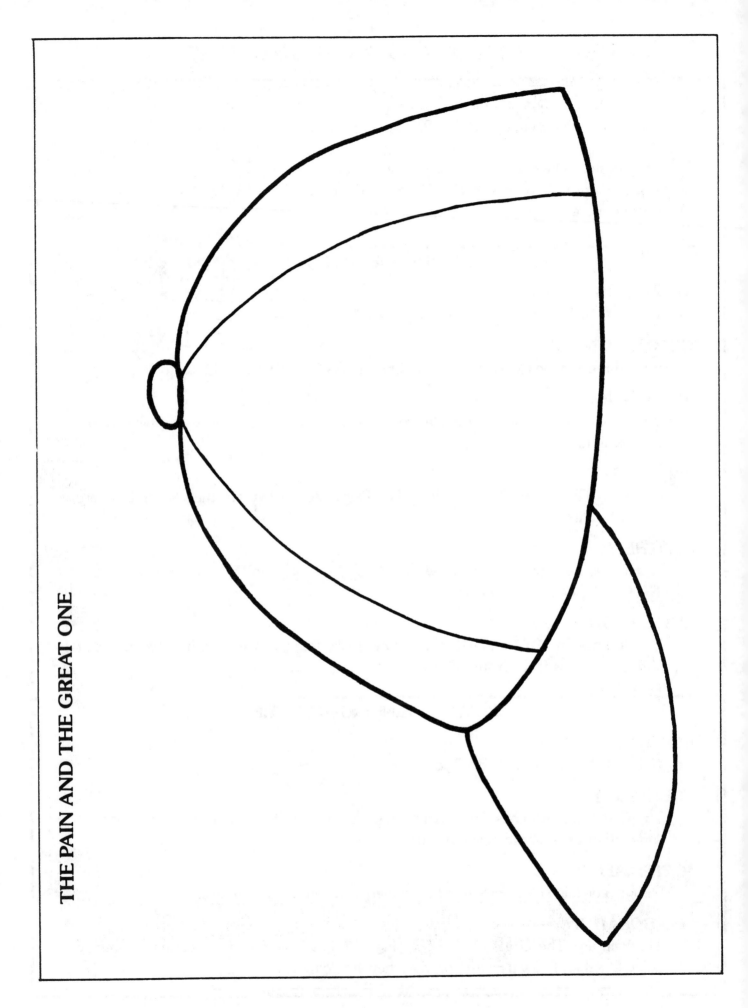

THE PAIN AND THE GREAT ONE

GA1164

Design a building block creation that someone
in your family can use.

Block Builder _____

79

The Pain and The Great One are
having fun playing together.
Draw a picture of what they are doing.

Play Supervisor _____

GA1164

THE PATCHWORK QUILT

Valerie Flournoy
Dial Books, NY, 1985

A loving relationship between a young girl and her grandmother is "spun" through a patchwork quilt.

BLOOM'S QUESTIONS

KNOWLEDGE
Describe the patchwork quilt.

COMPREHENSION
Why did Grandmother want to make a quilt?

APPLICATION
If you could make a special project with your grandma or grandpa, what would it be and why?

ANALYSIS
How is a department store quilt different from a handmade quilt?

*SYNTHESIS
Write a letter from Tanya to her grandmother expressing Tanya's feelings toward her grandmother.

EVALUATION
Evaluate the meaning of "a quilt never forgets."

CREATIVE THINKING ACTIVITIES

FLUENCY
Make a list of ways people record family memories.

FLEXIBILITY
Look at your list above. Rank your ideas from "most likely" to "least likely" to last several generations.

*ORIGINALITY
Design a patchwork square of your very own. Make sure it represents an event from your life.

ELABORATION
Elaborate on your patchwork square by attaching it to others in your room to form a "quilt." (Display your quilt squares on a bulletin board entitled "A Patchwork of Very Special Memories.")

GA1164

THE PATCHWORK QUILT

GA1164

Write a letter from Tanya to her grandmother.

Author _____

Draw a picture in the patchwork square representing
an event from your life.
Color a patterned design around the border.

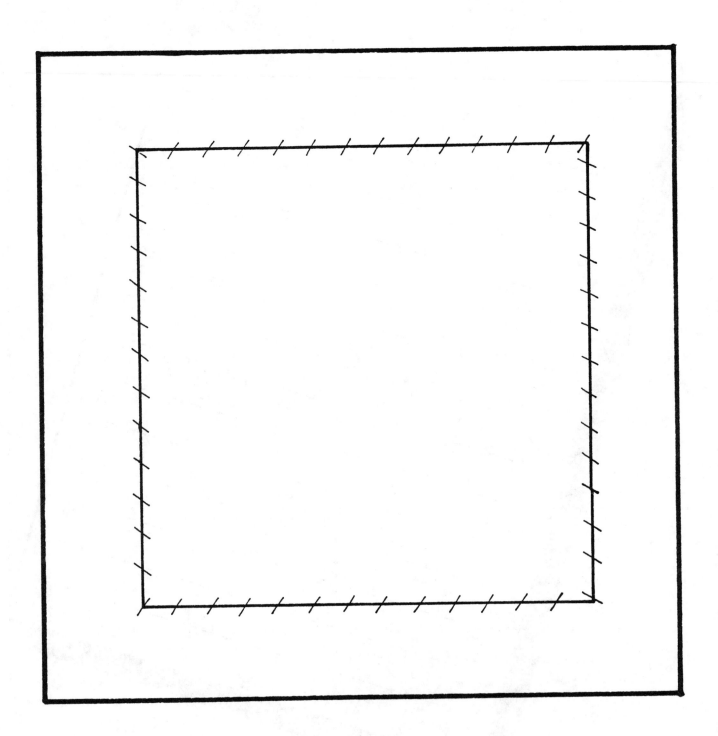

Quilt Maker _____

84

GA1164

PATRICK'S DINOSAURS

Carol Carrick
Clarion Books, NY, 1983

Patrick and his brother Hank spend the day at the zoo, where Patrick meets a variety of imagined dinosaurs.

BLOOM'S QUESTIONS

KNOWLEDGE
Tell what animals Patrick and Hank saw at the zoo.

COMPREHENSION
Why did Patrick want to go home after seeing only a few animals?

APPLICATION
Try to imagine what you would say if you were to meet a dinosaur on the way to school.

ANALYSIS
Compare and contrast a stegosaurus with a triceratops.

SYNTHESIS
What if the tyrannosaurus had entered Patrick's bedroom? Create a new ending for the story.

EVALUATION
Judge which dinosaur was most frightening to Patrick and tell why.

CREATIVE THINKING ACTIVITIES

FLUENCY
Make a list of words that can describe dinosaurs. Be creative with your answers.

FLEXIBILITY
Imagine that dinosaurs returned to the earth. List the problems the dinosaurs might encounter.

*ORIGINALITY
Create a T-shirt with a dinosaur design. Make it one you would be proud to wear. (Have students cut out T-shirts and hang in clothesline fashion across the room.)

*ELABORATION
Complete the dinosaur detective puzzle. Now imagine a walk through dinosaur land. Using the dinosaurs from the puzzle, describe in detail what you would find, who would be there, and how you would feel. Draw a picture of your dinosaur land.

PATRICK'S DINOSAURS

Create a T-shirt with a dinosaur design.

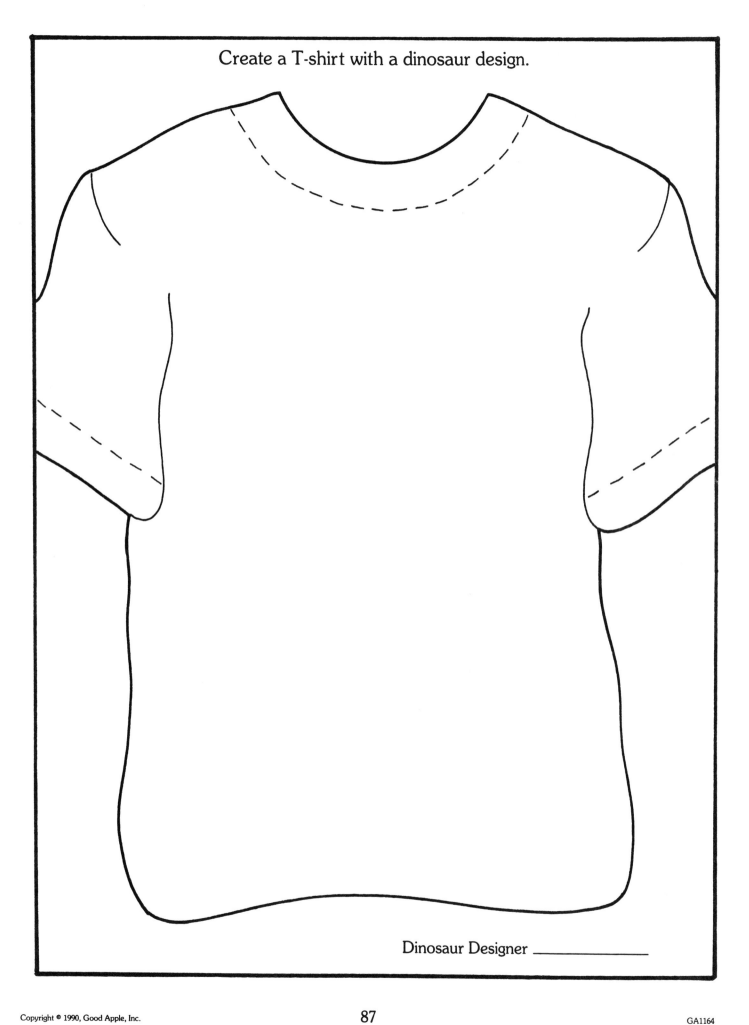

Dinosaur Designer _____

87

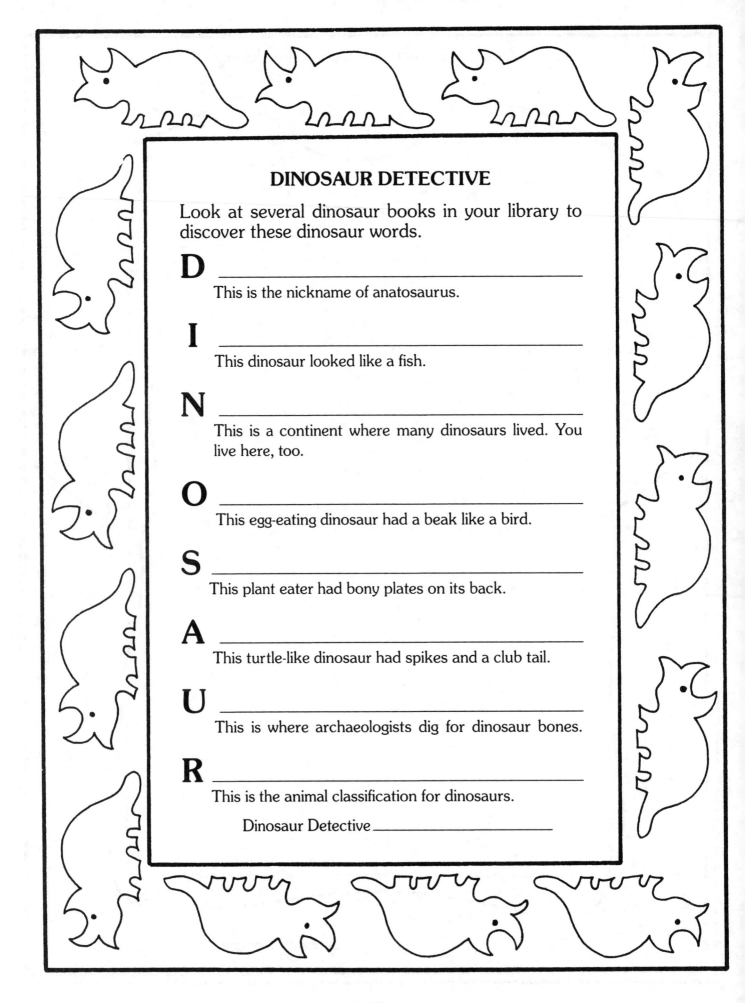

DINOSAUR DETECTIVE

Look at several dinosaur books in your library to discover these dinosaur words.

D _____

This is the nickname of anatosaurus.

I _____

This dinosaur looked like a fish.

N _____

This is a continent where many dinosaurs lived. You live here, too.

O _____

This egg-eating dinosaur had a beak like a bird.

S _____

This plant eater had bony plates on its back.

A _____

This turtle-like dinosaur had spikes and a club tail.

U _____

This is where archaeologists dig for dinosaur bones.

R _____

This is the animal classification for dinosaurs.

Dinosaur Detective _____

GA1164

ANSWER KEY

Dinosaur Detective

D DUCKBILL

I ICHTHYOSAURUS

N NORTH AMERICA

O ORNITHOMIMUS

S STEGOSAURUS

A ANKYLOSAURUS

U UNDERGROUND

R REPTILES

GA1164

Draw a picture of your dinosaur land.

Prehistoric Landscaper _____

GA1164

A POCKET FOR CORDUROY

Don Freeman
Viking Press, NY, 1978

Lisa loses her bear, Corduroy, in the laundromat. After much searching she finds him again.

BLOOM'S QUESTIONS

KNOWLEDGE
Where did Corduroy get lost?

COMPREHENSION
Describe how Corduroy spent his night alone in the laundromat.

APPLICATION
If you lost a stuffed animal, tell three things you would do to find it.

ANALYSIS
Compare Corduroy to a real bear. How are they alike? How are they different?

SYNTHESIS
Predict what would have happened if the man hadn't noticed Corduroy in his laundry bag.

EVALUATION
Consider what Lisa's thoughts were as she walked out of the laundromat without Corduroy.

CREATIVE THINKING ACTIVITIES

FLUENCY
List all of the things you can think of that have pockets.

FLEXIBILITY
What else could Corduroy use his pocket for besides holding his name tag?

*ORIGINALITY
Write an ad for Lisa to put in the Lost and Found section of the newspaper that will help her find Corduroy.

*ELABORATION
Add details to Corduroy's pocket to make it one everyone will want on his overalls.

GA1164

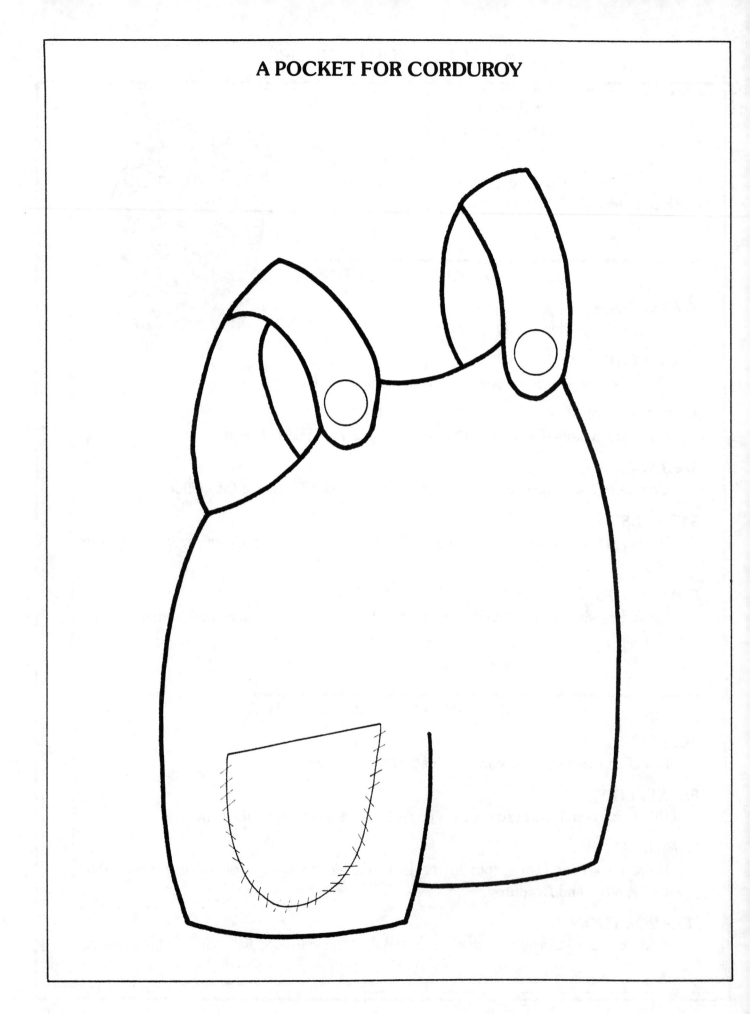

GA1164

Write a lost and found ad that will help Lisa find Corduroy.

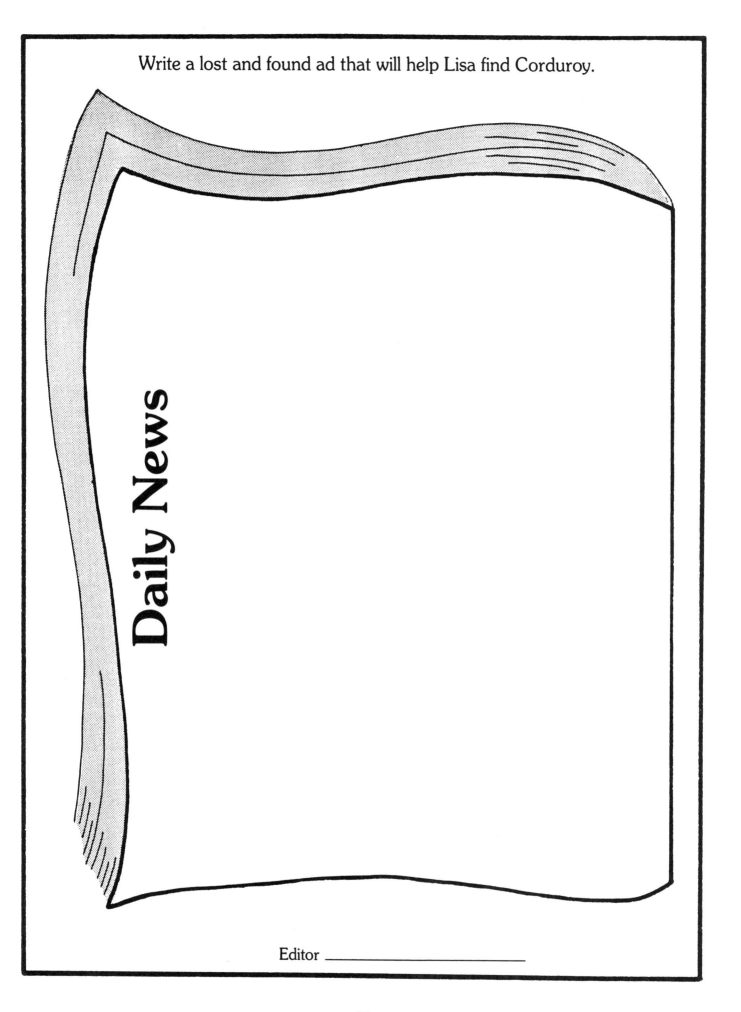

Daily News

Editor _____

Add details to Corduroy's pocket to make it one
everyone will want on his overalls.

Pocket Designer _____

94

THE RELATIVES CAME

Cynthia Rylant
Bradbury Press, NY, 1985

The relatives anticipate and share their annual summer vacation together.

BLOOM'S QUESTIONS

KNOWLEDGE

Where did the relatives live?

COMPREHENSION

Why was there so much hugging?

APPLICATION

What do you do when you visit your relatives?

ANALYSIS

Compare the activities depicted in the story with activities that may have occurred at a family reunion in pioneer days.

SYNTHESIS

Suppose all the relatives wanted to eat at the same time. How could they have managed this?

EVALUATION

Judge whether the relatives had a good vacation.

CREATIVE THINKING ACTIVITIES

FLUENCY

Make a list of things you see out the window as you travel.

FLEXIBILITY

Select five items from your list that are most commonly seen. Select five items from your list that are rarely seen.

*ORIGINALITY

Invent a new way for the relatives to travel to see each other. (Display the students' original travel ideas on a classroom mural.)

*ELABORATION

Fill the grocery bag with snacks and activities you would take on a trip.

GA1164

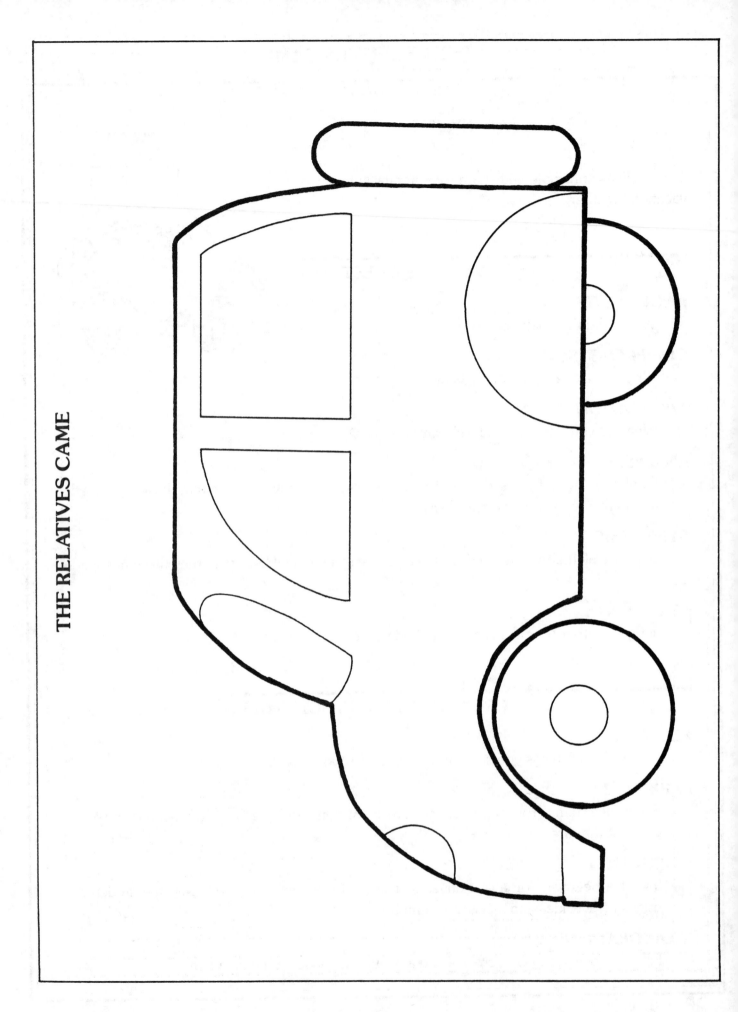

THE RELATIVES CAME

Invent a new way for the relatives to travel.

Travel Agent _____

Fill the grocery bag with snacks and
activities you would take on a trip.

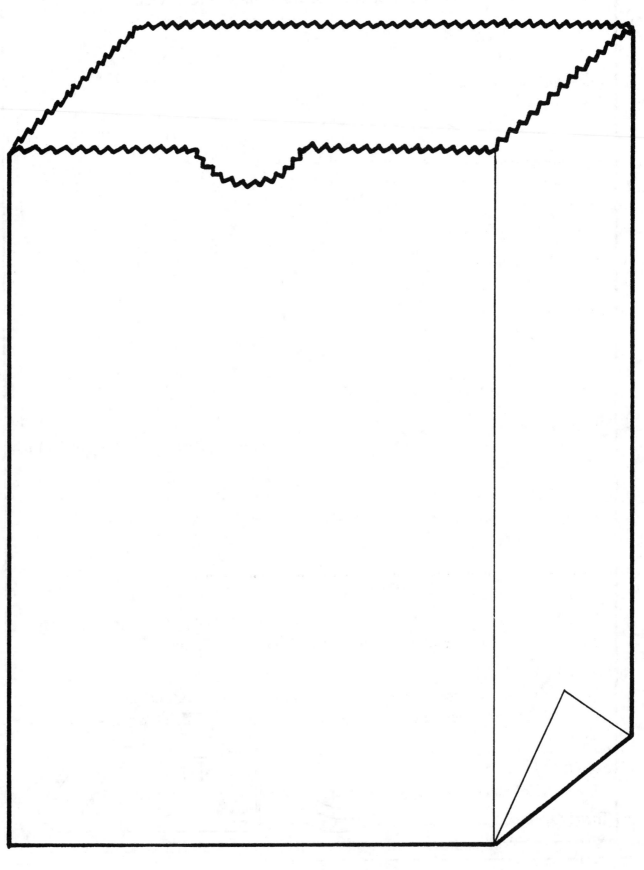

Bagger _____

98

THE SNOWY DAY

Ezra Jack Keats
Viking Press, NY, 1972

The Snowy Day is a small boy's story of his experiences on a snowy day.

BLOOM'S QUESTIONS

KNOWLEDGE
List the things Peter did in the snow.

COMPREHENSION
Explain why Peter didn't join the big boys in their snowball fight.

APPLICATION
If you were Peter, how would you have spent your day in the snow?

ANALYSIS
Compare a snowy day with a foggy day.

SYNTHESIS
Suppose the smiling snowman could talk with Peter. Role-play what they would say to each other.

EVALUATION
Choose what you believe to be the three best things that happened to Peter.

CREATIVE THINKING ACTIVITIES

FLUENCY
Make a list of all the things that you can think of to do in the snow.

*FLEXIBILITY
Look at your list of snow activities. Use the chart to categorize your activities into three groups: activities to do alone, activities to do with a friend, activities to do with a group.

ORIGINALITY
Create your own snow collage following the technique used by Ezra Jack Keats.

*ELABORATION
Elaborate on the end of the story—What did Peter and his friend do the second day in the snow?

GA1164

SNOW ACTIVITIES

ALONE	WITH A FRIEND	WITH A GROUP

Snow Buddy _____

GA1164

What did Peter and his friend
do the second day in the snow?

Storyteller _____

102

STREGA NONA

Tomie de Paola
Simon & Schuster, Inc., NY, 1975

Strega Nona has a magic pasta pot. Big Anthony discovers it and the whole town becomes involved.

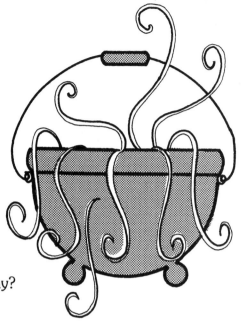

BLOOM'S QUESTIONS

KNOWLEDGE
Who were Strega Nona and Big Anthony?

COMPREHENSION
How did the people of the town feel about Big Anthony?

APPLICATION
Recite Strega Nona's chant to the pasta pot in our best magical voice.

ANALYSIS
Compare Big Anthony's disaster with the pasta pot to a "disaster" in your own life.

SYNTHESIS
What else could the townspeople have done with the pasta besides eat it?

EVALUATION
Do you think Big Anthony's punishment "fit the crime"?

CREATIVE THINKING ACTIVITIES

FLUENCY
Make a list of magic tricks you've seen performed.

FLEXIBILITY
Look at your list above. Choose which trick you would most like to learn and tell why.

*ORIGINALITY
Strega Nona had a magic pot. You have a magic tree. What will grow on it? (Laminate a colorful cover and make a class book.)

*ELABORATION
Look at the last picture in the book. Tell what Strega Nona and Big Anthony are thinking about.

GA1164

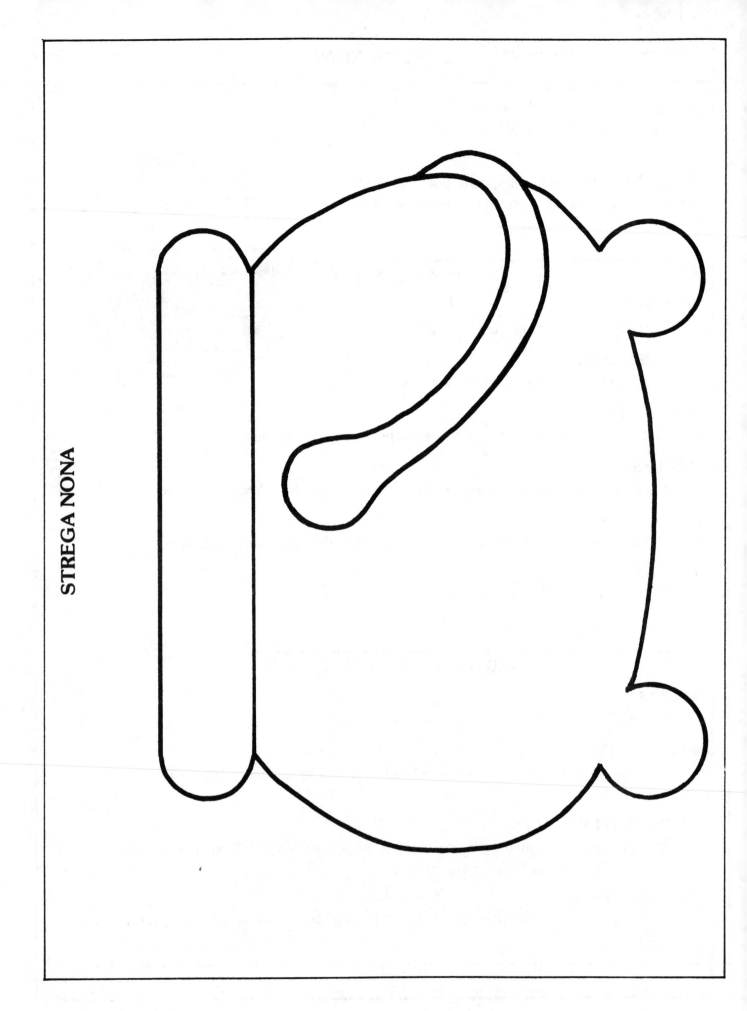

STREGA NONA

Magic Gardener _____

105

Tell what Strega Nona and Big Anthony
are thinking about.

Strega Nona

Big Anthony

Mind Reader _____

106

GA1164

SYLVESTER AND THE MAGIC PEBBLE

William Steig
Windmill Books, Inc., NY, 1969

Sylvester discovers a magic pebble. In a panic, he turns himself into a rock, unaware of the consequences.

BLOOM'S QUESTIONS

KNOWLEDGE

List four facts about the pebble Sylvester found.

COMPREHENSION

Describe the main events of the story in sequence.

APPLICATION

If you were Sylvester, what would you say to your parents when they found you? Role-play the scene where Sylvester's parents find him.

ANALYSIS

How is Sylvester's relationship with his parents like your relationship with your parents? How is it different?

SYNTHESIS

Suppose Sylvester had turned into a lake instead of a stone. How would it have changed the story? How would Mr. and Mrs. Duncan have found him?

EVALUATION

Write a short note to the author, Mr. Steig, explaining why you liked or didn't like this story.

CREATIVE THINKING ACTIVITIES

FLUENCY

Make a long list of wishes.

*FLEXIBILITY

Think of five extraordinary uses for a pebble or rock. Draw a picture of your favorite idea.

*ORIGINALITY

Create your own magic object. Draw it and tell about its magic.

ELABORATION

Mr. and Mrs. Duncan finally abandoned their search for Sylvester. Elaborate on other search methods they could have tried to help them locate Sylvester.

GA1164

SYLVESTER AND THE MAGIC PEBBLE

GA1164

Think of five extraordinary uses for a pebble or rock.
Draw a picture of your favorite idea.

Rock User _____

GA1164

Create your own magic object.
Draw it and tell about its magic.

Magician _____

110

GA1164

THE TENTH GOOD THING ABOUT BARNEY

Judith Viorst
MacMillan Publishing Co., NY, 1975

Barney, the cat, died and everyone was sad. Barney's family had a funeral and they remembered all the good things about Barney.

BLOOM'S QUESTIONS

KNOWLEDGE
Who is the main character of the story?

COMPREHENSION
Explain why Barney's family remembered good things about him.

APPLICATION
Draw a picture of your favorite memory of Barney, the cat.

ANALYSIS
Describe the relationship between Barney and his family.

SYNTHESIS
Create a Share Your Pet Day at school. Be ready to share three important things about your pet with the class.

EVALUATION
Judge who you think is the most understanding character in the story. Share your reasons.

CREATIVE THINKING ACTIVITIES

*FLUENCY
Create a pet booklet illustrating many kinds of pets.

FLEXIBILITY
Select your favorite pet from the booklet and write why you think it makes the best pet.

*ORIGINALITY
With a friend, write a cat song to sing at Barney's funeral.

ELABORATION
Create a list of ten good things about your pet or favorite stuffed animal. Use the same style as the author, Judith Viorst, does in the book.

GA1164

GA1164

Create a pet booklet illustrating many kinds of pets.

Pet Owner _____

Write a cat song to sing at Barney's funeral.

Lyricist _____

THE TERRIBLE THING THAT HAPPENED AT OUR HOUSE

Marge Blaine
Four Winds Press, NY, 1985

A young girl's account of her mother's return to work
as a science teacher.

BLOOM'S QUESTIONS

KNOWLEDGE
What was the "terrible thing" that happened in the story?

COMPREHENSION
How did the little girl feel about her mother returning to work? Why?

APPLICATION
Describe a time when something changed in your family and you didn't like it. How
did it make you feel?

ANALYSIS
Compare the little girl's activities before and after her mother went back to work.
How are they alike? How are they different?

SYNTHESIS
Predict how Mother's returning to work will affect the family on weekends.

EVALUATION
Decide if it was a good or bad idea for the mother to return to work. Explain.

CREATIVE THINKING ACTIVITIES

FLUENCY
Make a list of ways children can help out at home.

FLEXIBILITY
Look at your list and choose the five things your parents would find most helpful.

*ORIGINALITY
Draw a picture of yourself in your future career. Add as many details as you can.

*ELABORATION
Add your own personal information to the resume form. Attach it to your picture.
(Display the students' originality and elaboration activity sheets together to make an
interesting bulletin board.)

GA1164

THE TERRIBLE THING THAT
HAPPENED AT OUR HOUSE

Draw a picture of yourself in your future career.

Career Professional _____

A resumé shares your background, education, and experiences with a future employer. It helps you to get a job! Complete the following resumé about yourself. Simply fill in the needed information.

RESUMÉ

Name: _____

Address: _____

_____

Age: _____

Schools Attended: _____

_____

_____

_____

Other Activities: _____

_____

_____

_____

Jobs Around the House: _____

_____

_____

_____

Hobbies: _____

_____

_____

_____

GA1164

TIGHT TIMES

Barbara Shook Hazen
Penguin Books, NY, 1983

A small boy's father loses his job and the family experiences "tight times."

BLOOM'S QUESTIONS

KNOWLEDGE
What was the one thing the little boy wanted?

COMPREHENSION
Explain *tight times*. Use examples from the book.

APPLICATION
Describe a time when your mom or dad was sad. How did it make you feel?

ANALYSIS
What thoughts do you suppose the dad had as he walked home after losing his job?

SYNTHESIS
Create a special house for the little boy's new pet.

EVALUATION
Judge whether the little boy was understanding of his family's situation. Explain your answer.

CREATIVE THINKING ACTIVITIES

FLUENCY
Make a list of the things you would have to give up if your family experienced "tight times."

FLEXIBILITY
Look at your list above. What would be the most difficult thing to give up? Tell why.

*ORIGINALITY
Think of a terrific birthday present you could give your dad or mom that would not cost any money. Draw a picture of it.

*ELABORATION
Here is Dog's bowl. Add a design using a pattern or patterns to cover the bowl. Make it attractive so that Dog will be eager to eat her food.

GA1164

120

Think of a terrific birthday present you could give your mom or dad that would not cost any money.

Gift Giver_____

121

Add a pattern design to Dog's bowl to make it more attractive.

Dish Designer _____

THE VERY HUNGRY CATERPILLAR

Eric Carle
Collins Publishers, Cleveland, Ohio, 1979

The life cycle of a caterpillar is creatively explored in this colorful book.

BLOOM'S QUESTIONS

KNOWLEDGE
List all the food the hungry caterpillar ate in a week.

COMPREHENSION
Why did the hungry caterpillar get a stomachache?

*APPLICATION
If you were the hungry caterpillar, what kinds of food would you eat?

ANALYSIS
Compare the caterpillar with the butterfly. How are they the same? How are they different?

SYNTHESIS
Plan a well-balanced meal for the hungry caterpillar.

EVALUATION
Do you think it was a good idea for the caterpillar to eat so much food? Why or why not?

CREATIVE THINKING ACTIVITIES

FLUENCY
The very hungry caterpillar lives in a tree. Make a list of other animals that live in trees.

FLEXIBILITY
Are there any animals from your list that could be pets? Which ones?

*ORIGINALITY
The hungry caterpillar hatched from his cocoon. Suppose he had **not** turned into a butterfly. What do you imagine he turned into?

ELABORATION
Elaborate on the butterfly's adventures in the story. What else could have happened?

GA1164

THE VERY HUNGRY CATERPILLAR

124

If you were the hungry caterpillar,
what kinds of food would you eat?

Hungry Muncher ⎯⎯⎯⎯

GA1164

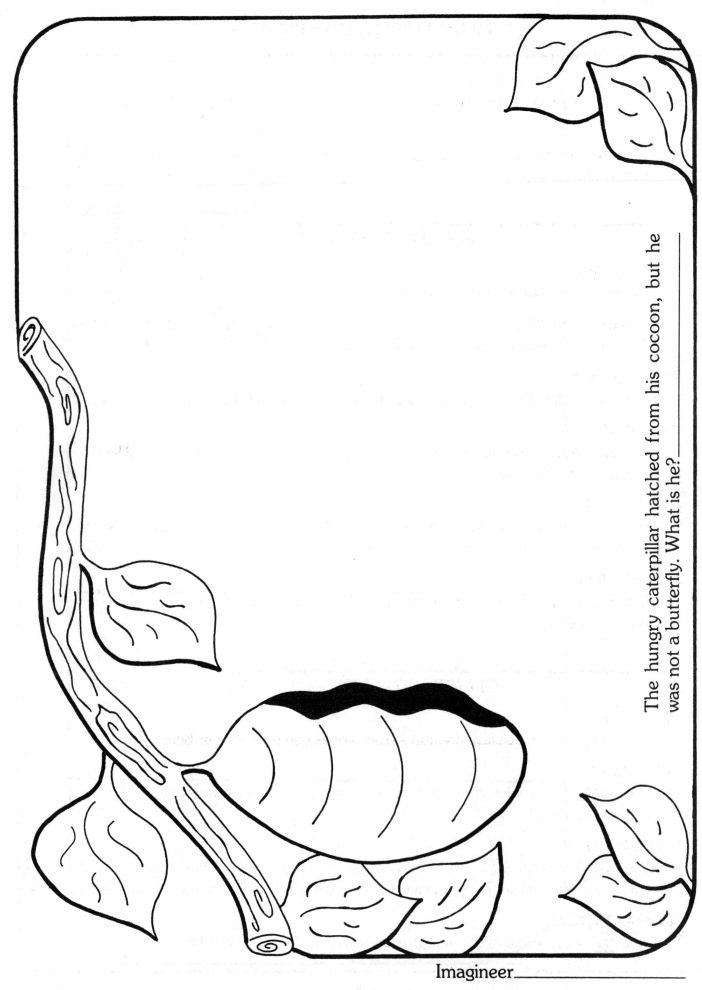

The hungry caterpillar hatched from his cocoon, but he was not a butterfly. What is he? _____

Imagineer_____

WHERE THE WILD THINGS ARE

Maurice Sendak
Harper & Row, NY, 1963

Max ventures into the land of Wild Things while being sent to bed without supper.

BLOOM'S QUESTIONS

KNOWLEDGE
Identify all the make-believe parts of the story?

COMPREHENSION
Explain why Max was sent to bed without supper.

APPLICATION
If you were Max, the Wild Thing, how would you say "I'll eat you up"?

ANALYSIS
Compare Max's wolf suit to the Wild Things he met. How do they look alike? How do they look different?

SYNTHESIS
Imagine what each of the Wild Things and Max are saying on the page after Max cries, "And now, let the wild rumpus start!"

EVALUATION
Is being sent to bed without supper a good punishment for acting like a Wild Thing? Why or why not?

CREATIVE THINKING ACTIVITIES

FLUENCY
Make a list of make-believe creatures from stories you have read or been told.

FLEXIBILITY
The Wild Things were great at creating a "rumpus." What else might a Wild Thing be great at doing?

*ORIGINALITY
Suppose you could be a Wild Thing. Draw a picture of what you would look like. Give yourself a "Wild Thing" name. (Display your Wild Thing in the school hallway.)

*ELABORATION
Add details to the curvy line and turn it into a home for your Wild Thing.

GA1164

WHERE THE WILD THINGS ARE

GA1164

Draw yourself as a Wild Thing.
Give yourself a "Wild Thing" name.

_____

Wild Thing _____

Add details to the curvy line and turn it into a home for your Wild Thing.

Architect _____

130

Bibliography

Allard, Harry and James Marshall. *Miss Nelson Is Missing*, New York: Scholastic, Inc., 1977.

Blaine, Marge. *The Terrible Thing That Happened at Our House*. New York: Four Winds Press, 1985.

Blume, Judy. *The One in the Middle Is the Green Kangaroo*. New York: Dell, 1981.

_____. *The Pain and the Great One*. New York: Dell, 1974.

Carle, Eric. *The Very Hungry Caterpillar*. Cleveland: Collins Publishers, 1979.

Carrick, Carol. *Patrick's Dinosaurs*. New York: Clarion Books, 1983.

Cooney, Barbara. *Miss Rumphius*. New York: Viking Penguin, Inc., 1982.

De Paola, Tomie. *Strega Nona*. New York: Simon & Schuster, Inc., 1975.

Flournoy, Valerie. *The Patchwork Quilt*. New York: Dial Books, 1985.

Freeman, Don. *A Pocket for Corduroy*. New York: Viking Press, 1978.

Gag, Wanda. *Millions of Cats*. New York: Coward-McCann, Inc., 1956.

Galdone, Paul. *Goldilocks and the Three Bears*. New York: Clairon Books, 1972.

Hazen, Barbara Shook. *Tight Times*. New York: Penguin Books, 1983.

Hoban, Lillian. *Arthur's Christmas Cookies*. New York: Harper & Row, 1972.

Hughes, Shirley. *Moving Molly*. New Jersey: Prentice-Hall, Inc., 1979.

Keats, Ezra Jack. *The Snowy Day*. New York: Viking Press, 1972.

Lobel, Arnold. *Ming Lo Moves the Mountain*. New York: Greenwillow Books, 1982.

McCloskey, Robert. *Blueberries for Sal*. New York: Scholastic, Inc., 1976.

Rylant, Cynthia. *The Relatives Came*. New York: Bradbury Press, 1985.

Schwartz, Amy. *Bea and Mr. Jones*. New York: Penguin Books, 1983.

Sendak, Maurice. *Where the Wild Things Are*. New York: Harper & Row, 1963.

Small, David. *Imogene's Antlers*. New York: Crown Publishers, Inc., 1985.

Steig, William. *Sylvester and the Magic Pebble*. New York: Windmill Books, Inc., 1969.

Van Allsburg, Chris. *Jumanji*. Boston: Houghton Mifflin, Co., 1981.

Viorst, Judith. *Alexander and the Terrible, Horrible, No Good, Very Bad Day*. New York: Atheneum, 1973.

_____. *The Tenth Good Thing About Barney*. New York: MacMillan, 1975.

Waber, Bernard. *Ira Sleeps Over*. New York: Scholastic, Inc., 1972.

Williams, Vera B. *A Chair for My Mother*. New York: Mulberry Books, 1982.

Wood, Audrey. *Heckedy Peg*. New York: Harcourt Brace Jovanovich, 1987.

Yolen, Jane. *Owl Moon*. New York: Putnam, 1987.